A Ministry Remembered

To Wayne & Deana from Joel

A Ministry Remembered

....

Dr. Fred Owen Doty

EDINBOROUGH PRESS

2009

Edinborough Press
  P. O. Box 13790
  Roseville, Minnesota 55117
  1-888-251-6336
  www.edinborough.com
  books@edinborough.com

The text is composed in Font Bureau Whitman and printed on acid-free paper.

Library of Congress Cataloging-in-Publication Data
Doty, Fred Owen, 1922-
  A Ministry Remembered / Fred Owen Doty.
    p. cm.
  ISBN 978-1-889020-31-0 (alk. paper)

Contents

In the Beginning

Old Hickory, Tennessee

Old Hickory, Tennessee—a mill town—population, 8,000—10,000.

No one lived in this little town other than the people who worked for Dupont Textile Industry. Schools, businesses, theater, houses, recreational facilities, grocery stores—everything belonged to Dupont or was leased out by Dupont.

There were schools and churches, separate ones for whites and for blacks.

There was a small village about a half-mile away called "Nigger Town." Dupont built and owned the houses the blacks lived in. The men from Nigger Town worked in the factory doing menial tasks. Many of the women were hired by white folks to do house work. There was no opportunity whatsoever for advancement for either black men or women.

White folks and blacks had little or no opportunity to talk to one another, to get to know one another, except for occasional, brief contacts in the grocery store and drug store.

This was the town in which I lived for all the years from early childhood until after I graduated from Dupont High School and went away to college, Duke University in Durham, North Carolina.

Looking back, I realize I was a sensitive little boy. My stomach tightened and my heart pounded when the boys in my neighborhood poured turpentine into the hole beneath the cat's tail, and laughed when the poor cat ran, scooting on its bottom in a frantic attempt to stop the pain. I didn't like it!

I didn't like it when the bullies were mean to smaller and frightened kids.

I didn't like it when the teacher scolded and spanked students in our class.

Most of all, I didn't like the way whites treated blacks, and no one could tell me why.

These feelings stayed with me all during my childhood and adolescence, and I can clearly remember the discomfort I felt when I came home from college one summer to see my family. When I opened the door to my home, the only person present was Lilly, an old black woman who was ironing some clothes. For me, she was a saint, if there ever was one. She had a lovely brown skin, thick grey hair and a warm smile that would melt ice. I loved her dearly, and I'm sure she knew it. The first thing I said to her in greeting was, "Oh, Lilly, sit down and have some lunch with me and tell me how things are with you."

From the look on her face, I could tell she was taken aback by my remark, and after a moment's hesitation she replied, "I'm so glad to see you, Mr. Fred, and thank you for inviting me to have lunch with you; but, you see, I cannot do that. I knows my place."

I grew to hate those words and what they implied, and still do to this day. You see, "Lilly" had a last name which I never knew, because she was never given the title of "Mrs." by a person whose skin was black, although she referred to me, always, as Mr. Fred, regardless of the difference in our ages.

Her place was subservient, initiated and continued by white folks. She learned it, and continued out of fear — fear of losing her job, or other even more devastating consequences. It did not feel good and right to me to be called Mr. Fred, so much younger and less experienced in life, when she was denied a true title of "Mrs." — a symbol of respect. It was demeaning to her, and it was demeaning to me, keeping me at arm's length from that saintly soul.

That memory quickened another that has stayed with me.

During the Second World War, I was attending Duke University, in the V-12 program of the U.S. Navy. My home in Old Hickory, Tennessee, was over 500 miles from the University. The buses were always overcrowded due to service men trying to get home "on leave", and with service men's wives and children attempting to visit their husbands and wives in the military.

One night I boarded a bus in Durham, North Carolina, headed for Nashville, Tennessee. I had scheduled the trip in the evening, hoping it would not be so crowded. Sure enough, there was one empty seat in the back of the bus, next to the section usually reserved for Negroes. I took the seat.

The bus stopped in every little town, and in one of the towns, a young Negro woman with a baby in her arms boarded the bus through the door at the back of the bus. She stood there and struggled to hold the baby with one arm as she reached for the belt strap with the other hand. The baby's whimpers were beginning to grow louder and little fists emerged from the pink blanket that had enfolded her.

I became uncomfortable immediately, observing how difficult this mother's situation was, especially when the bus would stop or slow down and she would almost lose her balance. I didn't wish to embarrass her, but I finally said, "Would you please take my seat so your baby can rest?"

"Oh, no sir," she replied, "I knows my place."

These words cut like a knife. Even though I had heard them before, and often, I still hated them. I tried again knowing she was having a hard time. "May I hold your baby so that you can rest a little and hold on more safely to the strap?"

She hesitated for a moment and then attempted to hold on with one hand and give me the baby with the other. I quickly reached up to receive the baby and hold her in my lap. I hoped that no "white folk" had noticed the transaction and cause trouble because I was having a conversation with a black woman and holding her black baby. Fortunately, no one said anything. I wondered if that young mother also feared someone would cause trouble and was relieved that no one did.

The mother could now hold on more carefully to the overhead strap. Occasionally she would touch her baby and talk gently to her as I moved the baby from side to side as she went to sleep.

Perhaps the white folk observing this scene had compassion for this young mother and her baby that transcended the learned prejudice against the color 'black'. Hopefully, they were relieved to see the injustice ameliorated, if only for a few moments. After all, this was a bus load of people going home for Christmas, a time of celebration for a newborn child.

Fortunately, the woman and her baby were traveling only a short distance, perhaps an hours' drive. When the time came for the mother to leave the bus she took her baby from me and took the first step off the bus. Then suddenly she turned around, looked straight into my eyes and said, with tears streaming down her cheeks, "I'll never forget you, sir. Never. Never!

Perhaps she will never forget the tears in my own eyes, knowing that some white folks were color-blind.

As I rode along in that bus through the mountains, that woman's face haunted me and I relived some of the injustices I had witnessed in my childhood. I wondered how it would feel to be home again.

I remembered when my hero, Joe Louis, was fighting the German fighter Max Schmeling. My father, my brother, and I were listening to the fight via the radio. My father and brother were yelling for Schmeling, the white man, and I was yelling for Joe, the American. At some point in the fight when Joe hit Schmeling with a flurry of left and rights, I yelled affirmatively for Joe. My father was furious with me, and yelled, "Go to your room!"

Frustrated and angry, I screamed, "I hope Joe kills him!"

My father started running after me; but he suddenly must have realized he would be missing the action, so he returned to the radio and left me to my room upstairs to lick my wounds. I learned the next morning that Schmeling had won, making things worse for me, but it may have saved me from a severe licking. Had Joe won, I would have been a target for my father's frustration.

I don't remember this specifically, but I imagine that I lay in bed, licking my wounds and consoling myself by feeling my father was prejudiced, and I was not! My feeling of moral superiority must have soothed my wounds, allowing me to fall asleep.

That was a painful memory for me, and I wondered if it were possibly painful for my father. After all, he was yelling for a white man, and I was strongly against a German. I realized in that moment, both of us were prejudiced!

That memory was followed by another of a hunting trip that I took with my father and my brother, Herb, who was two years older than I—a irritating problem for him. He didn't always want a little brother hanging around, tagging after him. He was a better athlete than I.

He was on the high school baseball, football, and boxing teams, while I was only on the football (second string) and the baseball team. By the time we were both in high school, however, we became teammates and cheered for each other in sports.

Another thing we had in common was our love of going duck hunting with our father. I sort of tagged along, whereas my brother was a good shot and often got his share of ducks.

One winter day, my brother and I became separated from our father, and during that time, Herb shot a male mallard duck and it fell about sixty to seventy feet out in the icy water. Silently we both looked at it helplessly, floating away out there; and then, out of the blue, Herb turned to me and said, "How about going out there and getting that duck?"

I was probably in junior high school, very much desirous of pleasing my big brother. Though the water was freezing cold with clumps of ice along the edges, out of my need to show my brother how brave I was, I agreed to go after the duck, and plunged in. This was obviously crazy behavior, but kid's needs are often so great they do crazy things. By the time I got to the duck and grabbed it, my body was icy cold and I found it difficult to turn around in the water that was up to my neck. After a struggle, I managed to turn around and face the shore. But with a dead duck clutched in my right fist, I couldn't move. I started to gasp and drop the duck when I heard Herb shout at me across the water. "Don't panic! Put the duck inside your shirt, and pull the water toward you one hand after the other!"

Gasping and gagging, I managed to reach the shore and tumble out, with my clothes not only soaking wet, but cold as the freezing temperature. Herb built a fire out of drift wood on the shore to dry my clothes, and while they were drying, he massaged my shivering body, skills he had learned in Boy Scout training.

We never told my father. We didn't dare. He would have been livid, and we dared not imagine the punishment. We both knew how foolish we had been, and it became our lifelong shared secret. I think it was probably harder on Herb than on me, because he was oldest and should have known better. Not that I also didn't know better.

My need to please almost ended in complete disaster. Realizing that, we never told anyone. It was our shared secret forever. Every once in a while the memory would surface, usually when we faced misunderstanding of one sort or another. That memory was a always a healer.

As these memories continued to unfold, I realized how powerfully my father loomed in so much of my life. Even the memory of my brother's and my secret played a powerful role.

One thing Herb and I always shared were those hunting trips with my father. We always looked forward to those trips, where we walked the fields and climbed the hills in search of cotton-tail rabbits, squirrels, quail, and other wild game. On one of these trips we happened to run into one of Dad's boyhood acquaintances. It was mostly small talk between them, until the conversation turned to immortality, and I became quite interested in the conversation. I was stunned when I heard the man say, "I shall never go to heaven, no matter what I do, for I have been condemned by God from the beginning of time to Hell and damnation, and there is no hope for me."

I do not remember my father's specific words in response, but I knew how he thought, and I can imagine him taking a long puff from his ever present cigar and say, "Well, I don't know where you got that idea, but that's not the God I believe in."

I thought about that man's words for along time. I was a very religious little boy and the loving Jesus of Nazareth was very important to me.

In my earliest years, I had found solace from the discomfort and pain of the everyday happenings in my life, not from what I learned during the week, but on Sundays. As far back as I can remember, my mother took me to Sunday School and church, and most Wednesdays evenings to prayer meeting. There was never any pressure. I wanted to go. The stories of Jesus of Nazareth touched my heart and Jesus became my hero. I wanted to be like Him; and, in looking back, it seems as though I always wanted to be a minister.

Jesus said, "Suffer the little children to come unto me." He said, "Come unto me all Ye that labor and are heavy laden, and I will give you rest."

I knew when I heard and read these words that he meant blacks as well as whites, and I loved Him for that. No way would the God that Jesus talked about condemn anyone to death. Where did that man get such a notion, I wondered. Probably from some wandering evangelist who had read the writings of John Calvin, who did believe in predestination by God.

Many years later, I learned in a Bible class at Duke University that, indeed, a lot of people had such beliefs, and that John Calvin and others preached such a doctrine. In the Old Testament (Exodus 3:19) it says that God hardened Pharaoh's heart, and yet punished him severely. It also said that God moved David to take a census and then punished David severely as well (2nd Samuel 24).

I also learned that Jesus rarely, if ever, suggests that the choices and acts of individuals are predetermined, though a few sayings may be taken to imply that the salvation of certain persons is divinely ordained.

But for me, the man Jesus was the one who said, "Come unto me all ye that labor and are heavy laden, and I will give you rest; the one who said to those who crucified him, "Father, forgive them, for they know not what they do." Even as a young boy, I somehow felt "called" to follow this man, Jesus.

In remembering these childhood experiences and thoughts, I realized that in my father's response to his old friend's ideas about predestination, on some level, without the education I was able to receive, my father had done his own thinking, and I began to appreciate him as I never had before.

It seems so strange that I would remember all these things on my way home again with my father in so prominent a role. No memory is more vivid than the Santa Claus memory.

I was a small boy during the depression, seven years old in 1929. I'm surprised at how much I remember. We could buy a loaf of bread for five cents, a gallon of milk for fifteen cents at the county dairy, if you brought your own jug. Eggs were 10 cents a dozen, and a number of companies made candy bars for a penny. At the end of the depression I distinctly remember selling a gallon of blackberries that I had tediously picked for twenty-five cents, and I felt I was rich. Sweets were rare and chicken on Sunday was a treat we all eagerly looked forward to. Macaroni and cheese was more nearly the order of the day. Many, many children went to bed hungry, and there were "soup lines" everywhere.

I still believed in Santa Claus when the depression came. But all that changed in a hurry. A few days before Christmas—a time we all eagerly awaited—my father called my brother and my sisters and me together and abruptly announced, "There is no Santa Claus." I believe my older brother knew. He sat there with a knowing look on his face as my father went on. "This year we don't have very much. We simply do not have it. Each of you can have one dollar. Spend it anyway you want to."

This was the first time I had ever seen my father cry. That was the worst pain of all.

We all knew that things were tight, but we didn't know what a burden it was on our dad and mother. A dollar to spend for each of us! That was BIG! I do not remember what my brother and sister purchased, but I remember what I bought, as if it were yesterday. I ordered it out of the Sears Roebuck catalogue for ninety-eight cents. It was a multi-colored, round top that had a fine point at the bottom. You pushed a button on the top as fast as you could, and the top went round and round faster then you could imagine. It was beautiful! And magical. I played with it by the hour, carried it around with me with pride, and even slept with it for a while.

Oh, yes, I forgot to mention, there was a stocking on Christmas morning, and each of us had more treasures—an apple, an orange, some dried raisins on a stem, and some hard candy. Once more, it was big time, and we made it last. I always kept the orange until all the other treats were gone. I wouldn't want to wish those days on today's children, but I would wish for them the gratitude we felt for those gifts, and for the knowledge that millions of children the world over would consider themselves wealthy to have what we had.

College and Seminary

The Journey Begins

From the time I arrived at school age, it seemed to me there was always someone who knew what I was supposed to be "when I grew up."

From the first grade on, my teachers, especially my math teacher in high school, thought I should be a math teacher because I was so good at it. My father said I should be a lawyer or a doctor. He scoffed at the ministry, saying that it was impossible to please everybody, and ministers didn't make enough money to keep body and soul together. The head of psychiatry at Duke University said a psychiatrist. Even though there always seemed to be someone who knew what I should be, for as long as I can remember, my heart said, "Be a minister." And I knew my heart was right.

But first, I knew I needed an education of the kind that would prepare me for the ministry that I felt so sure would fulfill my life.

And so, before I graduated from high school, I began to think about where I might go to college. I had no money. I had no help or guidance, either at school, or at home. Even though no one in my family, uncles, aunts, cousins, parents, or grandparents, had ever gone to college, it never occurred to me I would not go.

I applied to Vanderbilt (twelve miles from home), Southern Methodist, and Duke. I assumed it would be Vanderbilt, but they required two foreign languages for admission and only Latin had been offered in my small high school in Old Hickory.

Strange as it seems as I write this story, I had never visited Duke, I knew no one who had gone there, and knew nothing whatsoever about it, except hat they had a good football team and had played USC in a Rose Bowl Game.

So, I applied to Duke—and was accepted!

I had never even stepped on a college campus and had no clue as to the many worlds that awaited me at Duke University.

From the moment I entered the campus, I was stunned by the giant pines in the Duke forest and straight ahead the magnificent Gothic chapel, towering 210' feet into the heavens. All of the buildings were made of stone, and the Gothic architecture stunned my senses. It was all a shock to this eighteen year old from a small town in Tennessee.

Slowly, but surely, the greatest surprise were my professors, many of whom were giants in their professions, known and respected all over the world. When I casually remarked to someone how much I enjoyed my course in psychology, philosophy, religion, or political science, the response would follow, "That doesn't surprise me. He is one of the great professors in his field."

And so, the days, the weeks and months flew by and in March 1944, during my junior year, I entered the Navy V-12 program at Duke and my life changed dramatically. I was now in training to become a chaplain in the U.S. Navy program, and that meant finishing my A.B. degree at Duke, and another three years in seminary before I would be commissioned as a Navy chaplain.

My course work did not change, but everything else did change. Twenty-four hours a day my schedule and my actions were controlled by the U.S. Navy. The Navy decided when the day began, and when it ended; what clothes we wore, when we had a haircut, when we ate, the classes we took, and even our behavior in dorms. It was a also, now, a twelve-month program, rather than having summer months free from school.

It was difficult, but I understood why it had to be, and I was grateful for the opportunity to get my education, all expenses paid, and at the same time serve my country.

Mrs. Roosevelt

During my freshman year at Duke, a professor called me into his office and asked me if I would be interested in attending the annual meeting of the United States Student Assembly in New York City. The regular delegate was ill. I was a little intimidated at the thought of going to New York City and be the University's delegate to an organization about which I knew absolutely nothing. To say the least, the professor was persuasive, and I agreed to go.

Let's shift to a large meeting hall on a campus in New York City. For some reason, I spoke up on an issue before this large gathering. I had used the word 'Negra' (rather than Negro). Immediately some black student got up and accused Mr. Doty from Duke University as being prejudiced for misusing the proper pronunciation of Negro, and therefore discredited anything else I might have said. I was embarrassed and speechless, not quite sure how I had offended this angry young black student.

Hardly had the black student been seated when another student got up and said, "I strongly disagree with the accusation that Mr. Doty is prejudiced because he used the word 'Negra'. That's obviously what he learned in his culture. He may be prejudiced, but I have no reason to think so, and if either of these two men is prejudiced, I choose Mr. Doty's accuser."

There was laughter across the auditorium and the meeting continued. I forgot to mention that the student who defended me turned out to be a member of the Young Communist League, another organization about which I knew nothing.

One of the speakers for our conference was Eleanor Roosevelt, a woman very much interested in college youth and politics. She was definitely one of my heroes, and I was delighted when she was introduced. I have forgotten what she said, but I remember clearly that she cautioned us about underestimating the dedication and power of the Young Communist League. She said that while most of us would be relaxing when the meeting was over, frequenting bars and restaurants and having fun, the Young Communists would be hard at work and well into the night preparing to set forth an agenda for the next meeting, and we needed to be prepared.

The more she talked, the more upset I became, and when she asked for questions, I stood up and asked for the floor. She invited me to speak, and I told her that I objected to her criticism of the Young Communist League; and, in fact, what I heard, I liked.

Mrs. Roosevelt chuckled and remarked, "Mr. Doty, you remind me of Eleanor when she was a college student, spirited and naive."

You can imagine the laughter in the meeting hall, and once more my face was red. Not everyone laughed, however, and you can guess who did not laugh.

The last part of the conference was used to elect regional officers from all over the United States. The nominating committee had nominated a student from each region of the U.S. and now there were nominations from the floor. Usually the nominations from the committee were accepted, but a student waved for attention, and nominated Mr. Fred Doty from Duke University to be the regional representative from the South, and there was an immediate second to the motion. I was shocked, and before I knew it the vote was called—and Fred Doty — out of nowhere—was elected from the South!

As it turned out, the motion had been made and seconded by members of the Young Communist League, and they had voted in a block, and I was elected.

I don't know who the committee had nominated for the position, but whoever he/she was, would have been better qualified to be a member of the Assembly. Mrs. Roosevelt would not have been surprised. She would have seen me as someone the Young Communists could use to their end.

When I returned to the Duke Campus and the news came out in the *New York Times* of the election of regional delegates, the Duke professors, and others, were stunned. When they asked me how it happened, I probably said, "You won't believe it if I tell you."

Through the years I have recalled Mrs. Roosevelt's words contrasting enthusiasm and being informed. It is good to be enthusiastic, and it is important to be informed. I would clearly choose information without enthusiasm, rather than enthusiasm with naivete.

Thank you, Mrs. Roosevelt.

The Duke years were rich and full for me, and I will be forever grateful to my professors, to my classmate,s and to the U.S. Navy for making these experiences possible for me.

Yale University Divinity School

It was not until I went to seminary in New Haven, Connecticut, that I was in an integrated community. For the first time in my life I ate with blacks, worshipped with blacks, and played with blacks; and some of my friends roomed with blacks. I could easily have been assigned a black roommate.

Though it has been sixty years since I first sat down to dinner with blacks, I remember so clearly the Negro man on my left and the Negro woman across the table from me. Why am I crying as I write these words? I don't know. Was it the half truths, the lies that I had lived with all those years? The man on my left was dressed immaculately, perfectly groomed, spoke impeccable English, and seemed completely relaxed. He was warm, and cordial, with an engaging sense of humor.

The woman across the table was tall, thin, graceful, charming, and wore a long evening type dress that I was not used to seeing, even on a white woman. She was charm personified.

I quickly learned that the man, Bill, was the son of the president of a black college. My father was a mill worker with an 8th grade education from a one room school house in the hills of Tennessee. Bill had a beautiful baritone voice and sang in the seminary choir. You can imagine that I was all ears and eyes during that first meal with these remarkable blacks; and I had very little to say all during dinner. It was so unreal, so unlike anything that I had ever been told or experienced. It turned out to be transforming to body and soul. There were other blacks on campus, of course, and they added to this wonderful, integrated community.

One short story will suffice to represent the many stories which changed my life.

Late one evening, I walked by Bill's room and noticed that he was sitting at his desk with his head in his hands. I knew he had been crying. I crawled through his window and put my hands on his face.

He turned to me, and with tears in his eyes told me that he had been invited by a white friend to go home with him at Christmas time. The invitation had been cancelled by the white student's parents. Once more the evils of segregation had deeply hurt an exceptional human being who was paying a heavy price for being born black. I stayed with Bill, until his pain eased. He must have known I was hurting, too. That experience brought us much closer and we became good friends; not because of the color of our skins, but because we were soul mates. Years later, at a Yale reunion, I saw my friend coming up the hill towards the chapel. He recognized me at the same moment, started running, hooked his legs around my body and said, with a big smile, "How are you doing, Dotes?" (His nickname for me.)

That incident meant more for my southern soul than all the lectures by all the great lecturers on race that I had heard through the years.

Navy Shirt

Being sent to Yale by the U.S. Navy as preparation to become a chaplain meant that we were there, in uniform, for three years before we would be commissioned and assigned as Chaplain to some U.S. or foreign base.

We wore what appeared to be an officer's uniform, even though we were lowly apprentice seamen, the lowest rank in the Navy. We also had a white uniform for summer, and also a dark blue wool shirt with Navy buttons. I loved it and wore it one fall day to class. Just before I entered the building where my class was held, one of my professors abruptly stopped me and said, "Mr. Doty, this is Yale Divinity school, one of the most prestigious schools in America. You are fortunate to be a student on this campus. Your outfit this morning seems to me to be inappropriate."

To say the least, I was stunned. I recovered long enough to reply, "Yes, sir, I do feel most fortunate to be a member of this student body in a school where there is freedom to speak one's mind — as you clearly have — also free to decide what clothes one will wear. Respectfully, sir, you dress yourself, and I shall dress myself."

I walked away and into the building, down the hall and started to enter my class room. This particular class professor was the world-renowned church historian, Dr. Roland Bainton. Bainton's teaching of this class was legendary. This day's lecture was to be on Martin Luther, and I was very much looking forward to it. When I entered the classroom, Dr. Bainton saw my Navy shirt, touched it, and said, "What a wonderful shirt. Where did you get it?"

I explained that it was part of the Navy clothing. I unbuttoned it and handed it to him. He was terribly embarrassed and tried to refuse. I said, "You'll never know what it means to me to have you wear this shirt. You have made my day!"

And I walked into his classroom in my T-shirt and a smile on my face as big as Niagara. I left Dr. Bainton standing in the doorway with his Navy-blue wool shirt and a puzzled look on his face, saying, "How on earth did this happen?" After class I hurried to my room, (fearful I might run into the chastening professor) and dressed appropriately in another Navy Blue wool shirt.

To be honest, I hoped I would run into my well-dressed Professor, dressed only in my T-shirt. Then, I could say to him, "I'm sorry for being dressed like this, but Dr. Bainton was so impressed with my Navy-blue shirt, that I took it off and gave it to him. I'm on my way to dress more appropriately. (Sounds rather hostile, wouldn't you say?)

Damned For the Glory of God

Seminary was a great experience for me. My fellow students came from many denominations in the United States and around the world. Some were there to become university professors, some to become pastors, missionaries, college chaplains, armed service chaplains, etc. I was there to become a minister in a church.

One of my classes was offered to help us with writing sermons and preaching. Each member of the class had to deliver a sermon before the rest of the class. Some members of the class had some experience before coming to seminary, but most of us were "greenhorns" and nervous when our turn came. One member of our class was a bit of a character, quiet, a bit slouchy, and brilliant. He was one that people liked to tease. When his turn came to preach, he had everyone's full attention.

He had a long, easy gait, and it was amusing to see him walk down the aisle. He walked up to the pulpit and stood behind it, placed a hand on either side of it, leaned forward and said, "My reading is from John Calvin." There was a long pause, and then in a loud voice he exclaimed, "Damned for the glory of God, I'll be damned if I'll be damned for the glory of God!"

The class response was uncontrollable laughter, and that included the professor. The courage and the power of the speaker was a total surprise to everyone, including me, and I was his best friend.

When the laughter subsided, he continued his remarks, saying in essence, that no loving God as portrayed by Jesus could ever damn one of His children as suggested by John Calvin.

At the end of the sermon the professor's comment was, " Mr.——, all I can say is RAW POWER! " Once, more, a round of laughter and a round of applause.

A memory no one who attended could every forget.

A Favorite Teacher

One morning in my second year at Yale, I received a phone call from the secretary of the dean of students notifying me that the dean would like to see me. An appointment was set, but I had no idea what this meeting was all about. Frankly, I was uneasy and was glad when the appointment time came.

The dean began abruptly, "Thank you for coming, Fred. I will get to the point. Some years ago I was a student at Duke University, and during that time, I was a campus leader. I was president of the YMCA, an officer in my fraternity, a member of the speech team and held some other posts of leadership.

"Years later, you were a student at Duke, and interestingly enough, you were also a campus leader, and held the same offices that I had held when I was there. Now, both of us are at Yale Divinity School. Some other student was turned down for entrance when you were accepted at this special place.

He paused, as if not sure how to continue, and then said, "Fred, Yale deserves your best—if you are to stay here."

I broke in, "My grades are good."

The dean interrupted, "I know what your grades are. I want your best. Is that clear?"

I knew in my heart that I had been sluffing off a bit, too involved in extracurricular activities, so my response was swift. "Yes, sir, you will get my best."

The dean stuck out his hand and clasped mine firmly, "Good luck, Fred."

"Thank you, sir."

A favorite teacher cared enough to demand my best.

Heroic Professor

Through the years there are a few people that profoundly affect our lives. It may be what they say or what they do; how they treat us, or how they live their lives. They become our heroes and we may well try to be like them. For many of us, it is often a teacher. For me, there have been a number of them, dating all the way back to grade school. But one stands out like a beacon, a shining star, and his name is Richard Niebuhr, my Christian Ethics professor in seminary.

There were many things he said that I cherish and that will be a part of me always. We had an early morning class and when he entered the room, everyone became quiet. Rarely was anyone late. No one wanted to miss a word or to interrupt his class. He always began his class with a prayer and those prayers became legendary.

One morning was particularly moving. We clung to every word. It was not just what he said, but how he said it. There were no notes, nothing canned, just a man in search of his soul in our presence. The wrinkles in his brow were permanent, a witness to his life as a researcher. He had a profound respect for everything and everybody; and although he was a Christian, he brought us truths from many religions. On one occasion he said, "I am a Christian. I am a Jew. I am a Hindu. I am a Muslim."

There was not a dry eye in the room. We had the feeling that he had entered into the soul of the great researchers of all time. I truly believe that students of all religions would have felt at home in his classes. After that particular lecture, not a person stirred. We all sat quiet, mesmerized, stunned, humbled, and profoundly moved. Slowly, we exited, one by one.

As I remember, that was a Friday morning, and over the weekend there were lots of bull sessions in the dorms over what was said in Professor Niebuhr's class. It was a memorable class, to be sure, but what was even more memorable was the class that followed on Monday morning.

After he opened the class with prayer, he was very quiet. His head fell forward and with his hand on his wrinkled brow, he said, in quiet words, "Forget what I said last class. It's not quite right. Let me try again."

I thought I would choke. I could not hold back the tears, and I didn't care. Had he wrestled all weekend in the presence of God? That was Niebuhr to me and I worshipped him, the last thing in the world he would have wanted.

The statement he made that morning that exemplifies this spirit is, "I can always appreciate your affirmations, but I have trouble with your globalizations. When you say that my wife is beautiful, I can agree with you and rejoice with you. However, when you say my wife is the most beautiful woman in the world, I have trouble with that. Or when you say Christianity is a great religion, I can agree with you and rejoice in what it means to you; but when you say Christianity is the greatest religion in the world and the only way to salvation, I have trouble with that."

That principle has been a beacon to me in my ministry, a light that is needed as never before as our world becomes smaller and as more and more we live side by side. Like Niebuhr, we will profit from opening our hearts and minds to all of God's children. All of them.

The Divines

At Yale there were a number of divinity students in Navy uniform in preparation to become Navy chaplains. There were no Naval officers on the divinity school campus. Our commanding officer was a captain in the Navy and stationed in downtown Yale, about a mile from our campus. One of our Navy students was appointed a liaison between the Navy captain and students in training. One afternoon our student officer was going downtown to meet with the Navy Captain and those students.

After the student officer and the Captain had completed their business, we saluted him and he started to leave, then stopped and said, "By any chance can you Divines field a softball team to enter the tournament? You wouldn't have to win any games, but the other teams would see the Divines as regular guys. O.K?" My buddy and I looked at each other with big smiles, and I said, "No problem, Captain. I will organize a team, and we might win a game or two."

"Well," the captain said with a brief, disbelieving grin, "could be. You're on." And we were dismissed.

After the captain walked away, out of hearing distance, my friend "Chick" said, "Let's show them how to play soft ball, Dotes (everyone was using my nickname now). Chick (my friend's nickname) had been catcher for his college team, and I had played four years of High School baseball, and a lot of softball. Chick informed me that one of our divinity students from Wake Forest University was a super softball pitcher, one of the best. We passed the word around and ten guys turned out for our first practice. Chick had not been exaggerating. The 6' 3" pitcher was the fastest pitcher I had ever seen. We wet our lips in delight. We had seven excellent players, two guys were fair and one was okay. Our first game was against the Army Officers, and we slaughtered them 12 to 1. They were stunned, but we had expected to win. Word spread quickly for the other team to "look out for the Divines." We won every game handily, until the final game. We were to play another unbeaten team, and they were last year's champions. They, too, had a super pitcher, and a better balanced team than we did.

These were seven-inning games, and neither team scored for the first six innings.

In the seventh inning, I was the lead-off batter and lined a double (a two-base hit) into left center field. The next batter grounded out to second baseman, and I went to third base. We signaled the next batter to bunt on the third pitch, which would make the other team think we were not bunting. Our batter lay down a perfect bunt, and I went across home plate. It was the only score in the game and we were ecstatic. I don't know if our Navy captain and the other team thought we "Divines" were regular guys or not; but they discovered we had a whale of a softball team.

For a time, we put aside our divine humility—and gloated!

Internship

My experience in seminary prepared me well for the profession I had thought and dreamed about since I was a boy; but I had no idea what it meant to be in a real live church with its endless demands on a minister's life.

I was all set to take my first parish after graduation from Yale when I was invited to a one-year internship in one of the great churches in Protestantism, the First Community Church in Columbus, Ohio, where Dr. Roy Burkhart was the senior minister.

Dr. Burkhart had recently spoken at Yale concerning the ministry of his church, and I was tremendously impressed at the scope of the ministry as he had envisioned and developed it.

Actually, I was more than impressed, I was tongue-tied—a minister of children, a minister of youth, a minister of counseling, of music, of finance — all this, as well as a church camp on a lake in southern Ohio, with hundreds of youth involved—altogether a staff of thirty-seven.

When I found my voice after this wide-eyed excitement, my answer to this astonishing offer, was a resounding, "YES!"

The one-year internship extended to two years; and at the end of that time, I was invited to be the associate minister to Dr. Burkhart. Making that decision was the toughest of my young life, for I was sold 100% on First Community Church and its ministry.

After long self-searching, I said "no" to the invitation (much to everyone's surprise) in favor of a small, rural community church in Indiana, because that parish desperately needed a minister, and were hoping and praying I would answer their call.

There is no way I can ever repay Roy Burkhart and the staff of First Community Church for their love and support of me. That experience influenced my ministry for the rest of my years. Ministers would have stood in line for that position, but no one wanted that little church in Indiana. My decision was that simple, and my family and I moved to Chalmers, Indiana, in an old grain truck driven by a farmer and the principal of that little town's rural high school.

Through the years I experienced a great variety of situations. I served as an intern in a large suburban church with 5,000 members; in a small rural church in the Midwest; and in two very different congregations in Southern California, and as a mental health consultant in a Rural Hospital. In all of these situations, I found myself working with people of all ages, from birth until death; people with varying backgrounds—whites and blacks, orientals, Native Americans, lower middle class to wealthy. And in those rewarding years I learned that we human beings experience life in very similar ways.

We have dreams to fulfill, we fall short of expectations at one time or another. We know what it is to be lonely, to feel pain, to respond to acceptance and love; and we find criticism and rejection difficult to bear.

In every church I served, I sought to accept each person as a unique expression of the Creator, to be open to each person's need, and to love them for what they were.

It was not always easy, but it was amazingly transforming and rewarding.

The small rural church in Chalmers, Indiana was my first experience in the ministry entirely on my own, and with the unqualified support of my wife and many members of the congregation, it was an unforgettable experience.

As the years rolled along, I found the minutes, hours, days, years filled with amusing, joyous, puzzling, tragic times with this great variety of human beings all across America. Their stories are my ministry, and in remembering them and writing them down, and publishing them for you to read, it is my hope and my prayer that the stories will be meaningful to you as well.

Real Love

In my first assignment as Dr. Burkhardt's assistant, I made a get-acquainted call on a church member. I was warmly welcomed by her and one of her friends who was visiting with her. As the three of us got to know one another, I realized what a very caring person this parishioner was. She was attentive, she listened intently when others were talking; she evidenced a genuine concern for others, and she offered to assist me in making some hospital calls.

Just before I prepared to leave, I said, "Helen, you are a delight, and I am moved by your genuine concern for others."

Before she could respond, her neighbor spoke, "You have no idea how caring she is," and she related an amazing story. This neighbor had been through some difficult times, and was severely depressed, felt unloved and unappreciated, and wanted to die. Her energies waned and one day she collapsed and was rushed to the hospital. She remained in the hospital in a semiconscious state for almost a year.

She said, "Helen's minister asked her to call on me and every single day for a year she came to see me; yes, every day, rain or shine, winter or summer, holidays and all, she came. She talked to me as though I were awake, as though I could hear every word. She brought me news of my neighborhood, she told me what was happening in the U.S. and the world; she related news of her family and she read Bible passages that spoke of God's love. And she always touched my cheek with her warm hands when she entered and kissed my forehead when she left. Her final works were always, "And remember, God loves you and I love you."

By this time I was deeply moved, and I was wiping tears with a handkerchief. There was a long silence and she spoke once more. "I know it sounds crazy, and you must wonder how I knew Helen was there, but on some level I knew. And as the days and the months rolled by, I wanted her to come. I wanted to hear her voice, I wanted the warmth I felt when she was present. For a long time, I wanted to reach out and touch her, I wanted to say, "Thank you for loving me, I wanted to wake up and see her face."

At this point, we were all in tears and somehow we were in a circle of love embracing each other.

Finally she said, "You can see that I am well and I have been for a long time. I now know that I am lovable, that God loves me, and I'm surer than anything Helen loves me, and I'm so happy to tell you that I make hospital calls on the sick, taking a love that has been given freely and abundantly to me."

This story greatly affected my ministry for the rest of my active life, and many other forgotten souls found new life because of Helen's love that went on and on.

Rural Parish

Farmer's Family

My wife and I were having dinner together with the chairman of the pulpit committee of the Chalmer's church and his family. After a fabulous dinner and a tour of the farm, we sat down in the living room for a glass of iced tea The old farmer began the conversation.

"You and the Mrs. seem like such nice folk, and you surely have blessed our house with your presence this day. I guess you must know by now that all the members of the church are hoping and praying that you will become our minister. I don't know quite how to say it, but we kind of hope you will say 'no' to us. We don't want you to misunderstand, because we like you a lot, but this is a tough congregation to serve. It seems that everyone wants his way. They are always fighting about one thing or another, and I don't think the good Lord Himself could please them. What I'm trying to say is that we don't want to see you hurt. It doesn't seem right."

He was quiet for a moment and then added, "What has been said here is just between us and the Lord, if you know what I mean."

You can imagine how we felt as the old farmer and his wife opened their hearts so freely, trusting us to keep what they said to ourselves and the Lord.

That conversation took place more than half a century ago; and although I do not remember my exact words in reply to him, I do remember how I felt. I knew this dear couple were pure gold and that the congregation he was talking about really needing us. If I had any reservations about accepting the call, they were now gone. I sincerely felt we were the right fit for that congregation; and with others like this farmer and his wife, it was clear that they had a lot to give us.

Anyway, Jesus never promised his disciples a rose garden. We discovered that this couple was correct in that the thorns were surely there. We also learned that there were a lot of roses as well; and we seem to remember them forever.

Card Playing

One Sunday morning I was standing in at the door of the church, after the Sunday service, greeting parishioners. The next person in line was one of my deacons, and he greeted me with a smile and these words, spoken loudly enough for all his audience to hear, "Good morning, Rev. Fred; too bad you don't live up to those words you preached this morning."

"Sounds like you have some words you want me to hear, brother Bill."

"As a matter of fact, I do," he went on, "You know, we drive by your house when we go to town, and the Mrs. and I notice that you and your family play cards right in front of the of the window, in broad daylight. And you don't even pull the shades."

"You are right, Bill. I'm so glad you felt free to tell me what bothers you. We do play cards. We don't know how to play bridge, but we do play Rook with the children. It's a good way to teach them arithmetic. I learned how when I was a child, with my mother and dad and my brothers and sisters. We had such fun together. Perhaps you and the Mrs. would like to join us some evening. And, of course, we'll not pull the shades."

Bill had no further words and I added, "And thank you Bill, for having the courage to share your feelings with me. I hope you will continue to do that."

The next morning before breakfast, I responded to a gentle knock on our back door. When I opened the screen door, Bill was standing the there with a big smile. He spoke softly, "Brought you some fresh vegetables right out of our garden."

He hesitated, and then said, "Well, have a good day, Rev. Fred, and my regards to the Mrs."

It's been more than fifty years, but remembering Bill and his complaint, I'm guessing I have smiled and shed a tear or two.

I'm Going To Die

A minister's life is full of surprises. The very day we arrived in Chalmers, a phone call was waiting for me. The secretary said it was most important. So before we even emptied our suitcases, I made my first parish call. I was greeted warmly by an elderly woman who invited me in and immediately got to the point.

"I've been waiting for you to arrive," she said calmly. "I want you to have my service of memory (a gentler, kinder term for funeral). I knew when I heard your Easter service (the trial sermon before I was called to be the minister) that I wanted you to conduct my service. "I've lived a long and meaningful life, and I'm ready to go."

Quite surprised, I said, "I appreciate your kind words, but you appear to be very much alive and ready to live a long time."

She sat quietly for a long time, and then said, "Thank you for coming. My daughter will call you about plans for my service."

I called her by name, reached out to take her hands and said, "Thank you for this time with you. I'll call you tomorrow, and we'll talk again."

She smiled and took me to the door. As I walked down the street to the parsonage, I was bewildered. This amazing woman was gracious, warm, alive, most coherent , and yet she calmly said, "I'm going to die." How could it be, I wondered, and yet she seemed so sure.

At home, as we unpacked and attempted to put things in order, I kept thinking about that woman's words and wondered how I would respond to her tomorrow.

After a good night's sleep, I was awakened by the phone ringing. It was the woman's daughter asking me to call. I answered immediately. "Rev. Fred," she said, "My mother has just died."

A number of times in my ministry I have had similar experiences, and each time it was difficult for me. One woman was only forty-five years of age, looked great, had wonderful children, was financially in great shape, and felt loved by her husband and family. And yet, she too had said, "Rev. Fred, I'm going to die", and shortly thereafter, she passed away.

I discussed this with a doctor I admired, and he had similar experiences. He said, "Some live that I felt sure were going to die, and others died unexpectedly, when there was every sign and reason to live."

I have learned in my sixty plus years in the ministry to listen more, to have fewer answers, to realize my flock had much to teach me.

I also learned that it was more fruitful at times to listen together, rather than for me to pray aloud.

Shared Secret

My first parish was made up mostly of retired farm folk. A farmer's wife called one morning and said, "I want to come by for a few minutes and bring you some cherries." Her cherries were legendary in our town. As it turned out, she came for another reason also. She set the cherries on our kitchen table, and turned to me, with tears in her eyes.

"I've just learned that my husband has cancer, and the doctor said he may not have long to live."

Up to that day she hadn't realized his illness was so serious, and assumed he would be "up and around" in a few days. I had been to see him a couple of times and we had chatted about crops and the weather, about his wife's cherries—you know—small talk. I had no idea he was that seriously ill.

"What can I do for you? " I asked, shaken and heart-sick.

"Do something for him, please," she answered. "He told me just before I left that he would like you to drop by for a visit. That would be most helpful. But please—if you come, don't tell him that he has cancer. The doctor and I think it's better that he doesn't know, that it would upset him more than would be good for him right now. I want him to have these last few days in peace."

I thought I knew her husband fairly well, and I questioned her decision, but decided to say nothing until I talked to him. It was very tough news for her. They had a special relationship, and their marriage and been a blessing for both of them. She wanted to protect him from further pain as long as she could.

I called on him that same afternoon. I reached out my hand and was rewarded with that warm, gentle smile. "Thank you, Reverend Fred, for coming by. I have a favor to ask."

"What can I do?"

"Well, it's like this. I'm almost positive I have cancer and I do not have long to live. It's okay. I've had a long and good life, and you know a man couldn't have had a more wonderful wife than I have. She would only fret and fuss if I told her. I'd like to spare her as much pain as possible."

It was moments like this that made me a very rich man. Who else was so richly rewarded as to be able to share, in these rare moments, with this dear man and his wife. I took both of his hands in my hands, looked him in the eyes and asked, "My dear friend, do you trust me?"

"Why, what kind of a question is that, Rev. Fred. You know we both trust you and love you." Both our eyes were filled with tears.

"Then excuse me for a moment." And I went into the parlor and motioned for his wife to come into the bedroom, where her husband lay. "I want us to have a prayer together," and I took both their hands. "Thank you, God, for the wonderful life this couple have had together as man and wife." Still holding hands and looking into their eyes, I continued, "And I have a secret to share with both of you. I know something about you that you don't know."

I told them, then, what they each had told me, and when I had finished, they fell into each other's arms, and I slipped quietly away, leaving them alone together.

They kept in touch with me, and in the next few weeks they shared a most meaningful time together, as they had all of life from the day they were married.

Meddling

During the Korean War, I was still serving the small parish in rural Indiana, and a number of young men in my parish were in the armed services. I heard that some black marketing of fuel was going on in the area, and that one of my flock might be involved. I thought about it for days and days, and finally decided I needed to talk about it from the pulpit.

After all these years, I can't remember my exact words, but I talked about the war, and the sacrifices many people were making, especially those whose sons were overseas in Korea. I also said that each of us had a chance to support our troops with our thoughts, our prayer and our actions, and to use the war to "feather our nests" was a betrayal of our troops. There was a sober and quiet response as people filed out of the church.

A few days later, I decided to call on a man that I had reason to believe might be involved. I told no one about the call. I drove up to the farm and walked up the hill to his barn. He saw me coming. He picked up his pitch-fork and started walking toward me. My heart was pounding, and I was a bit concerned. When he came within about three feet from me, he raised his pitchfork and thrust it down into the earth about two feet from me.

In an angry voice he snarled, "Preacher! You've stopped preaching and started meddling. If you know what is good for you, you will back off!"

I was quiet for a moment, probably shaking a bit, and finally said, "This is not easy for me; in fact it is difficult for me to be here. You know how much I love your boys and . . . "

Before I could finish, he said, "Well, I'm sure you know they think a lot of you." "Yes, and I believe that if your boys were overseas fighting a war and someone was using it as an opportunity for padding his wallet and I said nothing, you'd wonder what kind of minister I was."

He was quiet for a while, and then he said, in broken words, "I, uh, guess you may be right, Reverend Fred, and I need to do something about it."

"Yes, I honestly feel you will, and I appreciate you hearing me out."

"I hear you like to rabbit hunt, Rev. Maybe you could come out some Saturday morning, and the boys will take you rabbit hunting.

Freckles

Most people in my rural parish in Chalmers, Indiana, were retired farmers or in business to service the farmers. There was no park or theater or gym, or anything for the young people except 4H clubs; and that wasn't for the kids that lived in town. I decided to organize a scout troop mainly for those town kids. Scouting had meant a lot to me when I was a boy growing up in Old Hickory, Tennessee. I had the needs of certain boys in mind.

Glen was about eleven years old and he and I and some of his friends were playing soft ball in a vacant lot behind the church. When the game was over, I slowly walked with him to his home. He had not played well in the ball game and he was a bit depressed. In fact, he was often "down on himself." He had said to me a few days earlier, "Reverend Fred, God pretty near (almost) ruined me, didn't He?"

"How so?" I replied.

"Well, just look at me."

Glen was short, thin, pink skinned and his face was a mass of large freckles. I was taken aback by his comment and replied, with my arm around him, "And one of the most lovable boys I've ever met." He responded with a half-smile and said, "Thanks for walking me home."

The scout troop was organized for the Glens of our little town and there were a number of them. The troop became a good one because I had found two other older guys to help me, and these guys really liked kids. One had been a scout when he was a boy.

Our troop had specialized in first aid and won awards all over the county. One of the best was Glen, and he was proud of his accomplishments. He and two others in our troop were chosen to attend a national

Scout Jamboree in the state of Washington. It changed their lives forever. When those boys returned and reported on their experiences, it brought pride to the entire town, and intense satisfaction to me and the other scout leaders. It reaffirmed our conviction that every child has a right to some personal skills that he/she can be proud of and that would enrich their lives forever.

O God, thank you for Glen, for his quiet manner, for his caring for his fellow scouts, for his trust of his scout leaders, for his humility in success, and for his child-like wonder in new experiences. And I thank you for the privilege of being a part of his life.

Lonely Men

Through the years I discovered that men would talk more than usual when they were hospitalized, flat on their backs, defenses down, afraid they were going to die. Often I would ask, "John, have you ever been angry with God?"

That question came because I sensed a deep down anger that never surfaced. Often these men immediately began to talk, saying things like, "Yes, I have. Because God isn't fair. He lets the mean person prosper, and the nice guy suffer; or He lets some people have health and our little son be born deformed. What have we done to deserve that?

One man said, "He seems to be there for the Reverend, but when I pray, He isn't there."

Another man said, "I prayed and prayed for our only son to be a good boy, but he has turned to drugs and he is always in trouble."

Another said, "He gave us a wonderful son and we loved him more than anything in the whole world, and God let him die when he was only twelve years old." Weeping, he added. "I just don't understand!"

Still another hospitalized man complained, "Why did God make me so ugly and my brother so handsome?"

There were many more who opened up and poured out their hearts, releasing deep feelings of anger and bewilderment that they had never been spoken of to anyone, not even to their wives. I cherished those intimate, painful moments with those wonderful men, finding an opportunity to relate on the deepest level, accepting their anger and bewilderment, sometimes crying with them—maybe the only tears shed as grown men—thanking them for their honesty, admitting the church had failed them with too easy answers to tough questions, sharing that even Jesus had moments of loneliness and felt forsaken by God, sharing a kind of love that they had not experienced in their church lives.

O God, there are times when life as one of your ministers has been a lonely one, times when I needed your presence, and like those men could not find you. But I am deeply grateful for the privilege of sharing your love with these lonely men in their difficult times. And for being there for me when I have taken the time to invite your presence. Amen.

Crazy Choice

When I left First Community Church in Columbus, Ohio for the small rural church in Indiana, many of my friends thought I was crazy. Shortly after my arrival, a number of my parishioners came to me with suggestions for getting members to come to church. A number of them said, "plant a garden, Reverend. Let the members see you in the garden when they ride by, and the word will spread that you are one of us." I don't know if those members actually rode by, or spread the word, but gardening was great fun for me, and we certainly needed the vegetables to feed all five of us, my wife and I, and three daughters.

One man said, "Brother Doty, I haven't had much luck getting my son to come to church, but if you would be willing to get up at four A.M. and run traps with him, I'll bet it would do the trick.

Did I hear him right? Four A.M.? But I think it will "turn the key". As you can guess, I made the call, learned about muskrat, mink, and other critters. Best of all, I got to know and care about a young farmer who began to attend church.

Another member said to me, "You know, Reverend, the local vet is having trouble getting someone to help him vaccinate hogs 'cuz all the young men are in the service." So you can guess, I became the one who held the squealing hogs while the vet "zapped them". It was a long day, and I wore the skin off my thighs. But the vet came to church to hear the gospel.

Another member came to me with his problem, "We need a third base-man. Can you play softball? (my great love). I joined the team and some ball players came to church and sat in the back pews, and also called for a listening ear when they were in trouble.

When Jesus said, "I call you to become fishers of men," he didn't say how many roads it might take to get the job done.

Dear God, Thank you for the incredible privilege of living day by day with those wonderful folks in rural America, running traps, vaccinating hogs, playing ball, wiping their tears, holding their babies in baptism, and loving them in joy, in anger and in pain. And "thank you especially for endowing me with the abundant energy to do all these things, and still be able to write meaningful sermons, at least some of the time. Thank you! Amen.

Conflict

Early in my stay in Chalmers, Indiana, one man was angry with me for inviting a Negro woman from Chicago to speak to my congregation. He met me on the street on Monday morning and said in an angry voice, "Did you not know that it is a law in this county that no Negro shall be in town when the sun goes down?"

I responded, "No, I'm not aware of that, and frankly I doubt that it is true; but if it is true, I shall begin this day to attempt to have it removed from the county charter."

This enraged him even more and he said, "How would you like to go out into the country and have it out?"

I said, "Start the car."

Apparently it surprised him and he responded, "Ah, hell, let's go across the street and have a cup of coffee."

I'm not proud of that story. I would handle it differently today, though it turned out okay and he and his family became church members.

I felt better about my comments when a fellow staff member who was upset with me challenged me to a fight. I said, "If that's what you want I will put on the boxing gloves with you and you will probably have the better of it; but when that is done, let's talk about the real problem."

I'm guessing that my voice was not hostile and that he felt my concern for he softened immediately and we began to address his anger and the pain and the fear underneath.

Years later, after my march in Selma, Alabama, a woman called me at 3 A.M., "Is this the goddam nigger-loving preacher?"

I replied, "You have that correct " and I added, "I want to commend you for having the courage to stay up until three in the morning and stand up for what you believe."

Stone silence, and then the click sounded as she hung up the phone.

It is quite obvious that the world does not have the answer to hate, either on a personal level, or on a group level. As has been wisely said, "The trouble with an eye for an eye is that it leaves all of us blind." Our current involvement in Iraq seems to have kindled flames of hatred the world over, so that even an eight and ten year old boy's dream in life is to kill Americans. I am ready to take a long and lasting look at the philosophy that would love enough to look beneath the hurt and the rage of enemies, to respond as I do to my own children and friends when they are upset with me; for to return hate for hate and bomb for bomb is a ticket for mutual destruction.

I know that response is an anathema to many Americans, whose diet since childhood is to meet the fist with a bigger fist, and the gun with a bigger gun. Jesus of Nazareth, Mahatma Gandhi, Martin Luther King, Jr. all died in defense of a better way. Father Elias Chacour of Palestine, who has suffered unspeakable injustice since childhood from the vindictiveness of his neighbors, is one living human being who has successfully returned love for hate. I'm ready to use what time I have left to resist the madness of "an eye for an eye and a tooth for a tooth."

I remember with humility when one of my children was enraged over something and banging away at one of her sisters. I felt for the sister who was being attacked, and didn't fight back and I asked, "Why do you let her get away with that?" She turned to me quickly in amazement and with eyes wide open said, "Daddy, can't you see she is hurting deep inside, and she certainly doesn't need me to attack her."

Once more, "And a little child shall lead us!"

Party Line

It has been over half a century ago since the time I served that small rural church in Indiana where most of my parishioners were farmers. It had been a new experience for me, and I loved it from the very beginning. It was a culture, however, like all cultures, that had its frustrating moments. There were no dial telephones, and most people were on party lines, meaning three or four may have had the same line, and any of these could listen in on others' conversations. I am not suggesting that everyone listened to others' conversations, but many did.

By the nature of my work, I found it frustrating to have other people listening in on conversations about personal church business, or personal situations in people's lives. I found it very difficult to talk with my family long distance in Tennessee, knowing that others were, or might be taking down every word. Many times I would drive eighteen to twenty miles to be assured of a private conversation.

After thinking about it a long time, I finally decided to be open and honest with my congregation and announced as a sermon topic, "Thou Shalt Not Steal." During my delivery, it soon became clear that I was not talking about chicken stealing, or horse thievery, or watermelon snitching, but stealing other people's personal and private thoughts and business.

Everyone knew what I was talking about and many agreed with my concerns; but the classic remark was made by the president of our church board.

As she was leaving the church, she shook my hand, straightened her shoulders, head held high, and said in self appreciation, "Reverend Doty, I'll have you know I have more important things to do than to be on the telephone all the time. I'll bet I don't listen in on other people's conversations more than an hour a day."

I thought I would die of laughter, but kept it all inside. She had been completely honest. Somehow the whole matter didn't seem to be so important after that. Of course, I was very careful, for at least an hour a day, about what I said on the telephone; and, incidentally, I was soon able to be the proud owner of a rare private line.

Transition

At the end of my fourth year in the Chalmers church, I received a call from the Lakewood Community Church in Long Beach, California, to become their minister of youth. I visited the church and was pleased with the philosophy and the direction of its program. The situation in Chalmers had become a good one, but my wife and I felt that we wanted our children to have greater growth opportunities in the schools, in the arts, and to be near to the ocean and national parks.

When we talked it over as a family, the lure of California won us over.

Personally, the chance to develop a youth program in a large church was especially exciting to me.

The Chalmers people were gracious and understanding and helped us get ready for our journey West.

California Parish

Synagogue Burned

One dark night the Jewish Synagogue not far from our church, burned to the ground and its leaders began searching for a temporary home for their religious services. Their main service was on Friday evening, and their education classes were held on Saturday. The rabbis and congregation were having difficulty finding a church that would accommodate their needs, and our congregation voted to invite them. It was an enriching experience for both congregations.

One day one of the Jewish leaders asked me if I would consider talking to their men's group on anti-Semitism. I thanked him and told him that I had a heavy schedule and didn't have time to properly research the subject. He said, "We don't want research, we want your own thoughts, your own experiences."

After a moment's reflection, my response came to me, "Well all right, if that is it. I kind of shoot from the hip talking with the guys—and if you don't bring your wives—I'll do it. Agreed?

Before the meeting date I reread a portion of Dr. Gordon Allport's *The Nature of Prejudice*, a section called, "Stereotypes of Jews." There were statements like, "They control finances and business, they are grasping and covetous, they are clannish, money is their god and on and on." I made a number of copies of the stereotypes and took them to the meeting.

When I got to the meeting room, I was surprised to discover that the room was filled and there were as many women as there were men. The men's leader was embarrassed and said simply, "They refused to stay at home," adding, "You know women, Dr. Doty." Hysterical laughter melted my frustration, and the meeting began.

Before meeting the group, I had asked a few Catholics and Protestants to mark the "stereotype statements" true—or false. I did not tell the group that I had done that. I passed out the sheet of stereotypes and asked them to mark them true or false. To everyone's surprise, the Jewish men and women had bought the stereotypes every bit as much as had the Catholics and Protestants. The meeting that followed was long and sober, as we realized how easy it is to be "bought by the lie" and controlled by it. We realized how much we needed each other, and that there was a lot of difficult work we needed to do together.

O God, how easy it is for us to be critical of others, to mouth half truths with little or no information. How often we project on to others what we dare not see . . . in ourselves. Help us to remove the "beam from our own eyes" before we criticize the splinter in our neighbor's eye. Amen.

One More Time

A beautiful young mother suddenly died leaving three little daughters and a bewildered husband. The mother and the little girls had come to church together every Sunday, and Dad had stayed at home—or wherever. I had finished my words at the service of memory, the mortician had closed the casket and the friends and relatives had filed out of the chapel. I was standing near the rear of the chapel as the father approached me and in a broken voice asked, "Could I please see her one more time?"

"Yes, you may," I answered, and together we walked to the front of the chapel, the mortician opened the casket, and the husband looked at his wife, tears falling from his eyes. He suddenly turned and hurried back down the aisle, and I quickly followed him. Suddenly, he stopped, turned to me pleading, "Please, please, please, just one more time."

I put my arm around his waist and we approached the casket again. The casket was opened a second time, and he stood quietly, tears falling, gently kissed his fingers and threw her a loving kiss. I gently led him away. We walked all the way to the back of the chapel, and he stopped again. I could see that pleading look in his eyes, feel the quivering attempt to ask, "One more time." I didn't wait for him to verbalize his deep wish and need to see his wife one more time. I led him back to the casket and there was a long, long squeezing of tears; and then, he straightened up, relaxed his muscles and said. "I'm ready to go now."

Later, after the committal, he said to me, "I don't find it easy to say what I feel. I've never gone to church, as you well know. My wife and the girls always go, It is important for them. And now I know why. I've experienced kindness and love here today in a special way."

He hesitated for a few moments, and then continued. "I'll be in church from now on and I'll bring the girls, and I thank you, Reverend Doty, more than I can say."

The mortician was frustrated at the delay in the committal, but he trusted me to help this aching husband with the most painful experience of his life.

O God, thank you for the capacity to feel and give love in times like these. And thank you for the love that will not let us go.

Suicide

I received a call one morning from a local mortician asking if I would conduct a service of memory for someone who had died. He sounded apologetic, but continued, "I know how busy you are, but—but I'm in a bind. You see, this is a suicide. I've called a few clergy and no one will conduct the service. One minister said, "God can forgive everything but a suicide." Would you be willing to take this service?"

"Yes", I answered immediately. "Of course I will conduct the service and the sooner I see the family, the better."

"They are here now," the mortician replied, "and as you can imagine, they are having a difficult time making decisions."

I met the family, listened a long time to their aching hearts, and we finally were able to make the decisions for the service and the care of the body. Some of the most sensitive members of my congregation who had gone through similar experiences answered my call for their help, and they faithfully stood by me as we guided the family through the troubled days ahead.

Later, the mortician asked me why I was willing to conduct this service for strangers, and to spend so much time with them. My answer was simple and clear. Suicides are almost always very painful experiences for the family. They are invitations for morbid feelings of guilt, for self-flagellation, for excessive drinking, for merciless condemnation of others, for cursing God as well as contemplation of other suicides by those who are left. And, believe it or not, suicides left without proper support and counseling can lead to suicides years later.

I told the mortician that my experience was that this is also a time of helping people to face and clarify their feelings, to deal with unanswered questions, to find guidance in understanding the difference between neurotic and normal guilt, to understand and accept the motive and action of the deceased. Most of all, it is an opportunity to clarify the power of God's love, and to help those left behind to move on with their lives.

Invaluable in these situations, is the presence of loving persons who have faced similar situations, and who are willing to help suffering families in these difficult times. It is not enough in times like these to say to the suffering, "I know how you feel." Often we don't have a clue. We need to listen, rather than to offer superficial answers. We need to lovingly stay close by as the healing process begins. It very often takes a long time.

Soul Food

Ellen was in the hospital, recovering from an illness. She hadn't been well since her beloved Ollie died. They had been partners for almost sixty years. I went to see her in the hospital, and she was glad to see me. She looked thin and frail, and as I hugged her I could feel the bones through her taut skin. When I released her I said, "Ellen, you're not getting enough nourishment."

"I'm not hungry, Fred."

Shortly, an orderly brought her evening meal. It wasn't the Waldorf, but it wasn't half bad. She took a bit or two and then pushed the food aside and said, "I'd much rather talk to you. Tell me everything that's going on in your life and at the church."

She obviously missed it. I began to feed her. She'd eat a few bites and then stop. We'd talk a little, and then a few more bites, until the food was all gone. When the nurse entered the room, she exclaimed, "My goodness, you ate everything!"

That's true, she did eat, but the food was incidental to her. She needed and "gobbled up" all the warmth and love she was missing. Every night, until she left the hospital, someone from the church was there to see that she had her physical nourishment, and to have the love dessert which she needed so much.

O God, thank you for the bread and the wine, for fruits and vegetables, for meat and potatoes, and for all that nourishes the body. And thank you for love and human warmth that nourish the spirit and keeps the inner person alive. Amen.

Tough Love

One day a young mother asked for some time to discuss a problem she was having with her son. She had been missing money from her pocket book, and she suspected her son was stealing from her. I suggested that she be positive that he was taking the money before she confronted him. She agreed to mark the bills and check his wallet when she missed the money again.

A few days later she called me and said some of her money was missing, and while her son was taking a shower in readiness to take his girl friend out to the movies, she found her marked money in his bill fold. I suggested she take the money and say nothing.

Her son, showered and dressed for the evening, came into the living room and said, "Goodbye, Mom." She answered, "Bye. Have a good time!"

When he came home later, she said, "How was your movie?"

"Lousy" he answered. "We didn't even go to the movie. When I got to the ticket window, I found I had no money. We went back to her house and watched T.V. I know I had the money. Someone must have taken it."

"I know what happened to the money," she said casually. "I took it."

"You took it!" he shouted in anger. "Why on earth would you take my money. I was so embarrassed!"

"I figured if you had the right to take money out of my purse without asking, I had the right to take money from your wallet."

Her son stomped out of the room as she sat crying. In a few minutes, He came back into the room, walked over to his mother and said, "I'm sorry for what I did. I was wrong, and I promise you I will never do that again. Not as long as I live."

As they hugged each other, she said, "I must tell you one thing more. I don't want there to be dishonesty between us. Your youth minister knows about this and he suggested I do that."

Her son seemed embarrassed, and took both her hands in his own. "Mom, it won't happen again. You may be sure."

Dear God, when I relive this story, I have a heavy heart. I ache for the boy and his girl friend. Even though the story seemed to turn out well, I wonder if I could not have found a better, more loving way to help that young man. What I suggested seemed right at the time. In looking back,

I remember his essential good-heartedness and emotional honesty. God, keep me aware that my good intensions, may be poorly carried out. Help me to take my time to think carefully before I offer clever advice. Amen.

Soldier's Boots

One Sunday morning—my day off from the parish—I went to answer the door and a man carrying a pair of heavy army boots stood waiting to see me. "Are you Rev. Fred Doty?" he asked.

"Yes, I am. That's quite a handsome pair of boots you're carrying."

"Yes, he said. "They belong to my son, but he won't be needing them any more." His voice was quivering, and he had trouble finishing his sentence.

"Won't you please come in?"

We sat down in the living room and I said, "I'm sorry, but I did not recognize you."

"Please forgive me. Of course you don't know me. I live a few houses away, but I am across that busy thoroughfare, the second house from the corner. I am Bill's father and your daughter Molly and Bill are best friends. I get the feeling that Bill spent more time at your house than he did in his own."

I interrupted, "Are you telling me that something has happened to Bill?"

He finally let me know amidst tears that Bill had been killed in a training mission near his army barracks overseas.

"Oh, my God," I responded, "what terrible news. How is your wife taking this?"

"Well, you can imagine that it's nothing short of a nightmare, and I'm worried about her."

I agreed to see his wife as soon as she felt ready. I told him that this would be a major shock for Molly, and for the whole student body of almost 2,500 students. Bill lettered in two or three sports and was everybody's friend.

As we were talking, I noticed the father kept his head down and was fiddling with Bill's boots. He finally looked up at me at me and said, "Would you like to have Bill's boots? I know it would please him if you wore his boots."

So painful even now to relive those moments. "I would be honored to wear Bill's boots. He was so important to us, so very important."

"I'm assuming that you would be willing to have Bill's service."

"Of course, of course; my privilege."

Then he said, "You know Bill never wore anything but brown khaki pants and a white t-shirt. He wore that combination as did a lot of his athletic buddies."

He hesitated for a moment and then asked, "Would it be disrespectful in anyway if the students wore khakis and a t-shirt at his service?"

"Not at all as far as I'm concerned. It will probably raise a few eyebrows and even a few criticisms, but I'll agree to that idea and handle the criticism.

Then he said, "One more question. Would you be willing to wear khakis and a t-shirt?" I hesitated for just a moment, and then began to laugh, and say, "Sure!"

The mortician was mortified that I would agree to such a request and he said, "Rev. Doty, I've never known a minister in my whole career who would wear khakis and a t-shirt at a sacred service."

I called the gentleman by his first name, and said, "I know, John, but it is not the ceremony that is sacred, it is the people and their wishes that are sacred."

There was a sea of high school youth, standing in the corners and not a chair was vacant. It was a love feast, and most people will remember, not what we wore, but what we shared. It was truly a service of loving memory for Bill, eased the pain a bit for those who loved and mourned him, and I feel sure Bill would have approved.

Woman in Hospital Bed

Many years ago I was taking a trip from Hollywood to pick up a car in northern California. I left early because I wanted to return the same day. My secretary reminded me that one of our church members was in a hospital in L. A., so I decided to stop by and visit her on my way north. It was early, but hospital patients are always up early. When I greeted my friend, she was so glad to see me that she put her arms around me for a big hug and shocked me with the statement, "Oh, Rev. Doty, I'm so glad to see you. I've been thinking about you a lot lately, and I want to thank you for all you've meant to me. The church had meant more to me than I can ever tell you."

She paused and then continued, "I'm going to die today, and I wanted to thank you somehow before I go. Now I can go in peace; and you can tell me you'll be willing to conduct my service of memory."

It's difficult, even impossible for me to remember my exact words, but I'm sure I held her in my arms, thanked her for her kind words and attempted to reassure her. Chances are ten to one, I had a prayer with her, thanking God for her wonderful life, for her love of life, for her concern for others. She changed the subject and asked me what I was doing in Hollywood—church was half an hour away—so early on Saturday morning. I told her I was going up north to pick up a car, and she replied, "Oh, well, I'll wait until you get back before I go."

Everything went well on my trip up north and I called on her again on my way home.

We had a short visit and she was as warm and loving as she had been earlier. When I got home my wife said, "Mrs. —— just called and said her mother had died and that she wanted you to have her service of memory. Though it was not the first time (nor the last) that this kind of thing happened in my ministry, I never seem ready to have it happen again. This woman did not seem at all a candidate for death. I would have been less surprised if she had said she planned to live to be a hundred. I told this story to a dear friend who happened to be a physician. He referred me to a book by another physician entitled, *The Will To Live*. The basic theme of the book was that individuals exercise a tremendous power over whether they live or die. This was a very important book for me, and I recalled, not only those people who had decided to die and were in seeming good health, but those who had decided to live when their physician had given them, at most, a few weeks to live. In the last few years, we have learned so much about the fact that life styles increase or decrease our years on this earth. Many have consciously altered their life styles and added to their lives; and others have continued to ignore the rules and added to the likelihood of an early death. Addiction to cigarettes and other drug substances are simple examples. I'm still humbled when I learn that someone in good health can will to die, and there is a powerful message for physicians and clergy to explore this mystery for the good of all.

You Don't Like Me, Do You?

I was in my office counseling with a man about thirty-five years of age. This was the third or fourth session, and we didn't seem to be going anywhere. I'm sure he knew it, and I certainly knew I was feeling uncomfortable as was he. All of a sudden he said, "You don't like me, do you?"

I wasn't prepared for that! What a lousy thing to say to your therapist. I had gone to college, to seminary, and I had my Ph.D. in psychology, but I wasn't prepared for this. I don't know how long it took me to recover, but words finally came to me. "I think we should find you another therapist."

It didn't work! He wouldn't let me off the hook. He asked again, and in a louder voice, "You don't like me, do you?"

I don't have any idea where my response came from, but with a deep sigh and in a subdued voice, I said, "No, I do not like you."

Before another word from me he shouted, "And I don't want another therapist. You don't like me, I don't like me, and I don't know anyone who does like me. At least, you were honest with me." The last few words were broken with tears.

I was half in tears myself, and said, "You know, I'm beginning to like you. Maybe we should begin to look at the things you don't like about yourself and see what you want to do about it."

He began to laugh then, and I began to laugh. And the therapy began.

I don't know what my mother would have said about this. She always said, "If you can't say anything good about a person, don't say anything."

Well, mothers don't know everything!

Great Men In Our Midst

Over the years I invited a number of great human beings, in many different fields to speak to my congregation. I wanted my parishioners to hear other voices, wiser, more experienced than mine. We received acceptances from a good number of the "Greats", Martin Luther King, Jr., Dr. Frank Laubach, Dr. J. B. Rhine, Dr. Paul Brand, Andrew Young, Lillian Smith, Robert E. Lee (writer of the Scopes Trial book) Millard Fuller, Louis Lomax, Dr. Roy Burkhart, and others.

One spiritual giant of our time was Dr. Howard Thurman, minister of

All-Peoples Church in San Francisco, and Dean of the Marquand Chapel at Boston University. He was invited to lead our congregation in a three-day spiritual retreat, and it was a highlight in our church's life.

A day or two before the retreat was to begin, one of my board members came to me in anger, saying, "You didn't tell me Thurman was black and I'm canceling my reservation."

I thought for a moment, then said, "I didn't tell you that Dr. Brand and Dr. J. B. Rhine were white when they came—nor will I do that. And you may cancel your reservation if you wish. A number of people would like to take your place. But I hope you will reconsider. You will miss the experience of a lifetime. We have waited three years to get into his schedule."

This man did change his mind, and said to me later, in tears, "I will never forget that experience as long as I live, and thank you, thank you for revealing my blindness."

Dr. Howard Thurman

Through the years in the ministry we meet a few great souls, persons who touch us deeply and influence our ministry forever. Such a person was Dr. Howard Thurman, Dean of the Chapel of Boston University and professor of spiritual discipline and resources in the School of Theology; all this as well as being the pastor of All People's Church in San Francisco. I first heard Dr. Thurman speak at the Yale Chapel when I was a student at Yale Divinity School. I did not hear him again for thirteen years, and that was in Los Angeles, California. I had used his books, however, in my small study groups, books that became favorites of many members of my parish.

Some of his book titles make you want to read his books, titles like such as *Deep Is the Hunger*, *Mediations of the Heart*, *The Growing Edge*, *The Inward Journey*, *Footnotes of a Dream*, and *Disciplines of the Spirit*. When I saw him again in Los Angeles, I invited him to speak in our pulpit, and to lead a three-day spiritual retreat in the Malibu Hills near the ocean.

I could see from his facial expression that he wasn't too excited about my request. He made it clear that his demands were great and his energies were limited. In so many words I said, "We can wait as long as we must wait."

"Three to four years?" he said with a gentle, loving smile.

"Yes, no matter how long."

And in three years we had a limited enrollment retreat, and those who attended it called it "the high point in their spiritual search." I share this story for a specific reason. Dr. Thurman spoke to overflow crowds at both our morning services. His energies necessitated that he speak only, and that I do the rest of the service. Furthermore, he was to rest (in my office) between services and he was to see no one.

At the end of each service, a number of people asked to see Dr. Thurman, and I explained his decision. Some were insistent to the point of being rude. Two or three insisted that I give him notes and wait for an answer. In each situation, he simply shook his head, "No."

It was quite obvious that a few people felt they were so important that he would say, "Yes." They left, angry with me and with Dr. Thurman.

When the second service was over and I had returned to my office, he seemed a bit rested. I told him that our people would be forever grateful, if he would just see them for a few minutes. He smiled and said, "You don't understand, do you?"

Near tears, I simply said, "No sir, I don't understand."

He leaned forward, and with that warm smile said, "Fred, it is really quite simple. 'Old Howard' knows how much energy he has, and I chose to be with you, not with them." And he added, "You did wait for me for more than three years."

Few words in my sixty years in the ministry have meant so much to me as, "Old Howard's energies are limited, and I had a choice." So much of my ministry has been controlled by the desire, the demands of the projections of other people. My neurotic need to please often left my energies depleted and my body ill. Too late in life I learned that I am not in this world to please others, but to discover who I am, to be true to that person, and to honor this blessed body that serves me so well. I am grateful that I am more in touch with my strengths and my weaknesses, and am able to make choices commensurate with that knowledge.

I thank you, Dr. Thurman, again and again.

A Dark Day Off

It was Monday, my day off—my time to relax, walk in the park, grocery shop, play games with my children when they came home from school.

I was dressed and ready to go out the door, when the telephone rang. I almost didn't answer it. I very much needed this time for myself. But something held me back. My parishioners rarely called on Monday, respecting my need for one day of privacy. So I turned around, went to the phone, and picked up the receiver.

A frantic voice, choked with tears, filled my ears. "Thank God you're home. Come to the house as fast as you can."

"I'm on my way," and I was out of the house with no questions asked. I knew the voice was Bill's, my gruff, no nonsense parishioner and L.A. police department officer. Bill lived a short three blocks away,

He was standing on the porch, waiting, sobbing, shaking, as I drove into the driveway. His arms opened wide to receive me and hold me close.

His sobbing seemed to have no end.

"Thank you for coming," he managed to say, without lifting his face from my shoulder.

"What on earth is the matter?" I managed to ask, my heart beating furiously. This behavior was unlike anything I could possibly imagine from the Bill I thought I knew.

Bill released me from the grip he held me in and opened the door. I followed him, heart pounding.

There on the floor was his tenth grade son, Brad, lying on his back, stiff as a board, head raised slightly, legs spread out as though frozen, hands, fingers spread and stiff, seeming to clutch the air.

Speechless, my own heart thumping wildly, I fell to my knees beside this silent, paralyzed young boy. Bill dropped to his knees beside me, and we wept together silently for God only knows how long.

After an eternity, it seemed, I broke the silence.

"Does your wife know?" I managed to ask.

"No," Bill responded weakly, "Diane's across the street having a cup of tea with her neighbor. I—I couldn't call her until you were here. I knew we would both need you. Fred, I'm afraid she'll go berserk. You see, I found an empty can of Pam beside him. We—we both knew he had been sniffing with some other kids, but I had warned him of the dangers involved and we both thought he had stopped. He—he obviously didn't get the message. Will Diane blame me for not watching him more closely when he went into the pool for a swim by himself? Did he have trouble breathing and tried to get out of the pool and call us for help?"

"I was too late—too late," Bill whispered as he put his face in his hands and his shoulders shook with silent sobs. I put my hand on his shoulder and let him cry. No need now to console him with empty words.

After what seemed like an eternity, we knew it was time to call Diane. We'd tell her I had stopped by for a few minutes to say hello.

Bill knew she would detect something from his voice—something wrong—and come right home. We covered Brad's naked body with a sheet, with only his face uncovered.

There is no way to adequately describe what happened when she saw her son on the floor, head raised inches, mouth open as though frozen in time. Her eyes shifted from Brad to Bill to me, back to Bill, again and again. Her muscles tightened, her head went back, her arms flung out and up, and she screamed loud enough to be heard across the street. She fell on the floor, draped herself across Brad's body, sobbing, "Oh, no! Oh no! Oh no!"

Together, both Bill and I knelt down beside her and held her, one on each side of her trembling body.

The next few hours were sheer hell. The next days were days of disbelief. The entire community was shaken to the core. I couldn't count the numbers of parents who identified with Bill and Diane and thought, "Oh God, it could have been my son!"

Neighbors and friends helped Bill and Diane and their children survive, but the memory of Brad's death will be remembered soberly, even after they may have moved far away from the scene of this tragic event.

Brad was not the only student who had been playing with death when they were sniffing inhalants. Brad's father knew this. As a police officer, Bill was very much aware of the temptation of sniffing and of drug use many young people fell victim to.

After a long, lingering period of grief, Bill decided, on his own, that he might make a difference in some lives if he spoke openly to High School groups of his own true life experience with this life-threatening habit. He decided to volunteer his time for this effort.

You can imagine how difficult this was for Bill; you can also imagine the power his message carried as the young people listened to Brad's father share his extreme pain when he shared his story of his much loved son's untimely and horrifying death.

There is no way of knowing how much value Bill's speaking did; but for him, it was a healing balm as his effort provided some hope that it would save the life of even one student.

Of course, I shall never forget that dark day-off. I experienced first-hand the heart-breaking dangers of sniffing inhalants. And I had the privilege of being there when truly needed.

I Want People To Like Me

I was a guest speaker at a church recently, and at the end of the service a young woman came up to me and asked if I could talk for a few minutes. As we talked I asked her what she really want out of life and she said, "I just want people to like me."

It was like a broken record. Over and over again I have heard people of all ages say, "All I want is for people to like me." As a youngster I wanted so much to be liked by others. I sought to please the adults around me, my father especially; and others, too, my teachers, my scout leader, my coaches, and my classmates. I would try to say what I thought they wanted to hear and do what they wanted me to do. I soon discovered that it was an impossible task, because what pleased one person, displeased another. It left me confused, not knowing who I really was, or what I wanted.

Through the years when I have asked, people to say to me, I have no idea who I am or what I want, because I have spent all my life trying to be what others wanted, or needed me to be.

Joseph Campbell, whom I met too late in my ministry, said, "Doing what someone else wants us to do is slave morality and a path to disease and disintegration of the spirit and the body."

He adds, "If someone tells us that we are selfish, it is often said because we are not doing what they want us to do."

I have come to the place where I am able to say, "I am not on this earth to please. I'm here to discover who I am, to find out what of the Creator is in me that is not in anyone else, and if I spend all my life in deifying another person's way, I'm ungrateful to my God and insult the gift of my own life."

I now cherish the words of Campbell, "The privilege of a life time is being who you are."

How sad it would be if we never heard the wild goose honk, because he wanted to be a cardinal, or a nightingale remain forever silent because she wanted to be like a chickadee.

What about our own deep love and truths. Following our own lives is not self indulgent, but rather honoring who we are and giving to the world the best we have to offer.

Says Campbell, "We can choose to live in rapture, and it is not out there in some other person or place or creed, but it is here within us."

Man and His Father

One of my parishioners made an appointment to see me about a personal problem. He had not had a good relationship with his father, and even though his dad had been dead for a number of years, he couldn't let his anger toward him go, and it was affecting his job and his marriage. I encouraged him to recall some of the events that poisoned his attitude towards his father. He spilled his guts, pouring out one complaint after another. This went on for one session after another, and I became concerned that his anger was destroying him.

The next time he came and started the pattern of attacking his father, I stood up, looked at the floor, and began kicking at an imaginary object. I said, "Damn you, take that and that and that."

I finally sat down, and saw that he had his head in his hands and was crying. I got up and started kicking again, and repeated the words, "Take that and that and that!"

Suddenly, he spoke, "Please stop, please stop!"

He continued to cry and cry. After a few minutes I handed him a box of Kleenex. He wiped his tears and I said, "I am so sorry you had a poor relationship with your father, and I wish we could change it, but we can't. I also wish your father could be here and would tell us about his relationship to his own father. My guess is that he suffered a lot of the same things that you suffered from him."

After a few moments of silence, I continued. "You need to let your father go; let him go. We may never know why you are mistreating yourself and your family. Perhaps you can even feel sorry for the little boy in your father who was so hurt and so angry that he unconsciously took it out on you."

I thought this hurting man would never stop crying; and after a time, I asked him to tell me about his son and his wife, and what he wanted to do to put his energies into those living relationships.

The healing began. And in time he was able to "let his father go" and to release the rage that crippled his own life and the relationship with his living family. Coming to grips with my relationship with my own father was most helpful to me in bringing relief to this man.

Letter to Father

When I was a child growing up I could never get enough time with my father. He worked every day and came home at 5:00, ate his supper, and usually went to his room and studied until bed time. He only had an eighth grade education and he was always trying to improve himself. It was clear to all of his family that he placed education as a high priority for himself and for his children.

On weekends my father liked to return to the hills where he grew up, and to go hunting with his old friends. He would leave early on Saturday morning and return on Sunday night. When my brother (two years older than I) was around eight years of age, my father would take him with him on these hunting trips. I wanted with all my heart to go with them, but my dad would say, "When you are eight years of age, you can come along." I watched in tears as they drove off.

My mother never criticized my father for not taking me with him, but she immediately found ways to ease my pain. Together we made candy, baked my favorite pie, played games, and I became her pal. When my sisters came along, I rocked them, fed them, played with them, which I actually enjoyed doing. This pattern continued through the years.

When I became old enough to go hunting, I enjoyed the trips, but the bond between my father and brother was very strong. My older brother was clearly my father's favorite; and I'm sure he felt I was our mother's favorite son. This pattern continued through the years, but gratefully we were able to resolve this conflict before he died.

I admired my father for so many reasons. He was a hard worker and gave his all to any job he tackled. He was honest in his dealings with people and his "word was his bond." And though he was not a churchgoer, he was a religious man and prayer was important in his life. It was my mother who faithfully took me to church.

While in college and seminary, I became more liberal in my religious, political, and social beliefs. I was especially opposed to segregation, and that was difficult for my dad. He thought I was too far to the left politically.

One of the redeeming factors in our relationship was hunting and fishing. We enjoyed walking the Tennessee fields and climbing the hills in search of wild game. One morning, with his back to me, he said, "If I had to do it all over again, things would be different." His voice cracked, and I knew he was trying to say, "I'm sorry."

"I know, Dad; I feel the same way."

It was a wild and windy day, and we wondered if we dared to try to put our little boat in the water. In macho fashion we did, one way of sharing a danger together.

Through the years in therapy, I tried to clarify my relationship with my father and take responsibility for my role in the alienation. I some how knew that in his own way, he had done the same thing.

When he died, the clergyman who was to conduct his service of memory became ill, and my brother and sisters asked me to conduct his service. My initial response was, "No way!"

After some deep thought and heartfelt discussion with my mother and my siblings, I changed my mind. It was very difficult for me and very healing. It was not a pious presentation, but an honest and soulful statement. My family seemed pleased. Thank God.

Later in my life, I wrote a long letter to my dad, saying some things I had never said to him in person. It was a very helpful thing for me, and I wish I had done it before he died.

Many times in my life, people came to me with problems with their parents. The fact that I had experienced the same things made me especially sympathetic, and I believe helpful. A number of men and women found that writing a letter to their parents, even after their death, and pouring our their honest feelings was most therapeutic.

It is never too late to write that letter! And be sure to have a box of Kleenex handy.

P.S. If you aren't going to be honest, don't waste your time.

I Goofed

I conducted a service of loving memory for my dear friend Terry, beloved by everyone in the congregation. He had lived ninety wonderful years, and I felt privileged to have shared many of those last years with him. The service was unforgettable because the sharing of his life had been so meaningful. Terry was a gentle, caring, bright, helpful, loving soul with a smile on his face that would melt an iceberg. Through the years he had served his fellow church members in endless ways. Terry would be forever remembered.

A few years later, I got a call from Terry's daughter-in-law, saying that her husband, Terry's son, had died and wondered if I would consider conducting his service of memory.

She said, "I'm not a member of your congregation, but I will never forget the service you had for our beloved Terry, and I know Ellie (Terry's wife) and the family would be pleased."

I, of course, agreed. I called on her in her home, listened to her memoirs, and we planned the service together, including the poetry, the music, and the scripture that she wanted. She gave me the freedom to add other things that I felt would enrich the service.

At the close of the service, I walked down to where she was sitting, to take her hands and lead her our of the sanctuary. What I saw stunned me—a cold, ashen, angry face, and a pulling back, refusing to let me touch her. One of the family led her out of the church. Never in my ministry had I been so shocked. What on earth had I done? When the friends had expressed their condolences and I could attempt to talk to her, she screamed at me, "For God's sake, you had the entire Bible for references, why did you have to include that pagan poem? I was in poor shape, trying to understand her fury and in some way bring her some calm in this painful moment. The pagan reference she referred to was from William Cullen Bryant's *Thanatopsis*. The specific passage was:

So live that when thy summons comes to join
The innumerable caravan which moves
To that mysterious realm, where each shall take
His chamber in the silent halls of death
Thou go not like the quarry-slave at night,

Scoured to his dungeon, but sustained and soothed
By an unfaltering trust, approach thy grave
Like one that wraps the drapery of his couch
About him and lies down to pleasant dreams.

It was poetry that I had used in other services, poetry that I had heard others use, and always with appreciation. That wasn't the point, it was the wrong choice for her, and she never forgave me. I wrote to her, apologizing for not checking my choices before the service, and then called her on the phone. She closed all doors of communication.

Her mother-in-law, Ellie, said to me in her gentle and loving way, "Darling Fred, let it be just, let it be."

After forty years, as I relive this story, my body trembles, and my eyes fill with tears. I learned from that awful experience, there would be times when "the walls come tumbling down" and I had to "let it be in the hands of God." I also learned to check my choices more carefully in the future.

God Came To Me Last Night

A church in southern California called a special meeting to discuss whether one of the ministers should be rehired. A number of people felt it was time for him to leave and there were those who wanted him to stay. There was to be open and honest discussion and an unbiased moderator was chosen to supervise the discussion.

The moment the chairperson called the meeting to order, the minister in question rose to the floor and said, "Mr. Chairperson, this meeting is unnecessary because the Lord came to me last night in a dream and said I was to stay."

The moment he sat down, a woman stood up, asked for permission to speak, and said, "The Lord came to me last night and said, "Rev. —— is to go." There was laughter everywhere and the meeting continued.

Through the years I have known people who appeared to have a special line to heaven. God seemed always to say what they wanted and agreed with their point of view. I had trouble with that. It certainly was not my experience. My experience was more like the psalmist when he said, "How long will you hide your face from me? Will you forget me forever?"

Or the author of Psalm 22 who said, "My God, my God, why have you forsaken me. Why are you so far from helping me, and from the words of my groaning? I cry out in he daytime, but you do not hear, and the night season, and am not silent."

Even Jesus did not seem to have an open line himself to God, and once in agony he cried, "My God, my God, why have you forsaken me?"

And Job said, "If he goes by me, I do not see Him, if He moves past I do not perceive Him." The God of the psalmist, the God of Job, the God of Jesus does not seem to be available at the snap of the finger! Even Jesus searched long and hard in the desert for inner peace, for clarity of mind, and for a sense of direction.

"Be still and know that I am God" has been a guide for me, a discipline that takes time—lots of time.

Breakfast with Nelson Rockefeller

It was in the middle sixties, and the civil rights movement was very much alive. John Kennedy had barely edged Richard Nixon for the presidency. The key civil rights leaders were pressuring Kennedy to take a more bold stand on civil rights, and he was trying to steer a middle course, wishing to cooperate with the civil rights leaders and not wishing to alienate the southern white voters. Very outspoken concerning the rights of the Negro was the powerful Republican, Nelson Rockefeller.

One morning I received a call from a member of the local Republican committee in Woodlands Hills, California, the parish I had been called to from Long Beach, asking if I would like to have breakfast with Nelson Rockefeller of New York.

"Thank you, but I think not," I said, picturing a large group of politicians, each trying to find time with Rockefeller.

"Fred", my friend said, "there will be maybe ten or twelve people at the breakfast and Rockefeller wants to meet you. You're the only Democrat that's been invited."

"You're kidding," I lightened up. "Why in the world would he want to meet me?"

"He's heard about your inviting Martin Luther King to your pulpit and he knows you marched in Selma. He's very much interested the civil rights movement."

"Well, well, well! I'll be there for sure."

I was seated next to Rockefeller, and he was a charmer, delightful. He really was interested in the civil rights movement, especially in Martin Luther King. Some of his family was active in the movement, especially with Dr. King, and if I remember correctly had participated in some of the marches.

I learned later that he had given thousands of dollars to the Southern Christian Leadership Conference. Some said he was simply seeking the Negro vote when he planned to run against John Kennedy the second term.

To my amazement and delight, I had more time with Rockefeller than anyone else at the breakfast table. At one point, with a boyish grin, he said, "I don't suppose you would vote for me for president?"

With a hearty laugh, I remarked, "Stranger things have happened, but I will follow your campaign closely. I'll be interested in what you say, and why. If you are everybody's man to win votes, I'll not be interested. I'm basically a Democrat and not a big business man whose main interest is money, and who cares little for the common man except to use him for his own ends."

"Wow," Rockefeller said, "that's pretty nasty."

"Yes, it is nasty, but I believe it's true. I am delighted that you seem to care about King and the civil rights movement, and I don't believe it is just to get the black votes."

He responded warmly, "Thanks, Fred, keep up the good work. I've enjoyed our time together."

"Likewise, and I'll be watching and listening."

If I Had Only

Four friends and I were on a canoe trip into the Canadian Northwoods. The area called the Quetico is legendary for its beauty, its wildlife, its solitariness, and its opportunity to catch fish. We found all those things to be true. We had been bathed in beauty, we had seen bear on the trail, heard the haunting calls of the wolves and the loons, and been awed by the sight and the sound of the mighty moose. And dare I mention that we had caught more fish than any of us had thought possible—bass, perch, northern pike, lake trout, and the enviable walleye.

We were so deep in the wilderness that we rarely saw anyone, not even an Indian. We were to be in the woods for almost two weeks. Occasionally, we would hear a helicopter, or hear a voice sending a message to whom, we did not know. Days later, when we arrived at a lodge near our journey's end, someone asked us if one of us might be Rev. Fred Doty. I said, "Yes, I am Rev. Fred Doty."

I was told to call home at once. I learned that my beloved choral director had died, and that they wanted me to conduct his service of memory. What a shock! As I learned during the phone call, he had died shortly after we had entered the Quetico. and a minister friend had conducted the service of memory.

As soon as we returned to California, and I had removed my thirteen-day-old beard, I called on my choral director's wife. We visited for a long time about her long life with her beloved Jay, and his lifetime career in choral music. More than once, she used the phrase, "If we had only . . . " done this or that, and now it was too late. Time after time in my ministry at some one's death, I've heard the surviving spouse repeat those words. "If I had only, or if we had only." My wife and I are now in the twilight of our years, and we know too well the sadness of those words. Already five of our dearest friends have died this year, and we know too well the sadness of those words, and it is only the month of June.

The poetic words, "Come live with me, the best is yet to be, the last of life for which the first was made" are tempered by "If I had only." More and more, Kathy and I are substituting the "tomorrow" for "today". Now is the time to say "thank you" or "I'm sorry." Now is the time to say "I love you, or "please forgive me". Today is the day to write the letter of appreciation, to send the roses, to take the trip.

Perhaps what I am trying to say can best be expressed from the poem "Look To This Day" from the *Sanskrit*:

Look to this day for it is life, the very life of life
In its brief course lie all the verities and the realities of your existence
The bliss of growth
The glory of action

The splendor of beauty
For yesterday is already a dream
And tomorrow is only a vision
But today, well lived, makes every yesterday a dream of happiness
and every tomorrow a vision of hope.
Look well, therefore, to this day
Such is the salutation of the dawn.

Damn Your God

One of my parishioners was in the hospital for cancer and both of her breasts had to be removed. When I went to see her, she screamed at me "Goddam your God!"

Her eyes were wide open, her muscles were tight, and she shook with rage. I sat down beside her and said to her, "Say it again, say it again, say it again."

She seemed shocked at my response, and began to sob and moan, squeezing out the pain and the sorrow. Finally, amidst her tears, in broken words she said, "Oh. Rev. Doty, I'm sorry, so sorry."

"Why are you sorry? Those precious breasts, a part of you femininity, gone forever."

"Why wouldn't you be angry? I'm guessing you've been proud of those breasts since you were a young girl. Your breasts have been a meaningful part of who you are as a feminine human being, both for you and your husband."

"Yes, yes" she cried softly.

"I'm angry, too, that these things happen, and I cannot imagine you not being angry."

We sat in quiet and I held her hand. Then I asked her, "Do you blame God for your cancer? Do you think he should interfere and cure your cancer? Should He take away all illness?"

"Oh, Reverend Doty, I'm so confused and so sorry that I blew up at you."

"My dear ——, I'm grateful that you did exactly what you did. You were honest with me, and I'm proud of you."

She closed her eyes and cried softly saying, "Why, why?"

I wept openly with her and said, "Oh God, I wish I knew, I wish I knew."

I shared with her the words of Jesus to His disciples in the garden of Gethsemane when He said in pain, "Couldn't you have watched with me for one hour; and His agony at His crucifixion, 'My God, my God, why hast Thou forsaken me?' "

I confessed to her that the church had been far too glib and simplistic about its answers to the problems of suffering, and that we needed to be more honest and open as she had been with me. I left that day with the words, "I'm sure of one thing, the God I know loves you and would never in a million years take your breasts away."

We had subsequent visits, and she became the one I called on to meet with and counsel with women in the church who had breast operations such as hers. The sharing of the women eased the anger and the sorrow of their loss. And I was grateful.

I Forgot

Minister's meetings can be productive, they can be boring, and sometimes they can be fun. One of the funniest I ever attended was a meeting where the guys (no women ministers at that meeting) were sharing embarrassing moments in their ministries. Actually, when the events happened they were far from funny; but later, remembering them, sharing them, became a way of reducing the pressures we were all very often under. Almost every one of us had been late, or simply had forgotten an important meeting. A number had forgotten a wedding, and one had forgotten a funeral (right time, wrong date.)

I have been in the active ministry for about sixty years. Even today, I am not infrequently called upon to perform a wedding service or conduct a funeral service, I like to call a "service of memory."

As long as I can remember, I have had anxiety over the possibility of forgetting an important meeting or appointment or service. Even though a secretary or other helper would make a note for me on Friday afternoon before leaving the church, I knew I could possibly forget to look at my appointment book. To this day the anxiety manifests itself in dreams in which I forget some important meeting or appointment or service, or am unprepared for some special presentation.

One Saturday afternoon, after a morning of making unexpected calls, I went to my church to pick up a book. I was dressed in khaki pants, a T-shirt, and sandals. When I got to the parking lot next to the church, I noticed two couples getting out of their car and walking toward the chapel. I recognized one of the women. She was dressed as a would-be bride.

"Oh, my God, it has happened to me!" I was supposed to be performing a wedding ceremony in about ten minutes! I hurried home (two miles from the church) faster then the speed limit, quickly changed my clothes and zoomed back to the church.

I approached the two couples. They seemed as relaxed as could be. The bride smiled at me and said, "John thought you might have forgotten, but I assured him that you would never forget our wedding."

"Thank you, Mary, for your support. I'm sorry I was a bit late and scared you. My schedule was brutal today."

All went well, thank God. There were no wedding guests waiting outside the locked church door. I almost never had a wedding with only the bride, bridegroom, best man and maid of honor.

To this day, I don't know whether they really thought I had forgotten their special day. However, when the groom handed me the envelope with an honorarium, I handed it back to him with, "Thanks, but no thanks." I felt as though I should have given him and honorarium.

Believe it or not, ministers have considered leaving the ministry for forgetting events that simply must not be forgotten; until they are, of course.

Death of a Student

I was working in my office one morning around ten o'clock when my secretary interrupted me. She told me to pick up the phone because a young woman seemed quite upset. When I answered the phone, the woman was in tears and asked if I could come over right away. Her husband was a junior high teacher and she said he would be there also. I left immediately. When I got to their home, I found her husband sitting in a chair, leaning over with his head in his hands. He was visibly shocked and didn't lift his head or say a word.

The woman began to talk, "We just learned that our seventh grade son died in the nurse's office at school." Before she could finish, I said, "My God, how did it happen?"

She continued, "At first I was shocked, and then my neighbor—she's very religious— said that God wanted our son more than we do, and that He had called him to heaven to be with Him; and I can accept that. I feel better now that he is with God."

Her husband lifted his head, sat up straight and as she talked he seemed to become more and more angry. He began to pace the floor. Then his wife asked me. "Rev. Doty, do you agree with my neighbor?" Her husband stopped his pacing, looked at me, seeming to be waiting for my answer. I didn't wish to upset her temporary calm, nor hurt her neighbor who was trying to help her with this sudden, dreadful shock. But I knew there was no way I could accept her neighbor's answer, no matter how well meaning. So I said, "I am glad you were not alone when you learned about your son's death, but there are a number of things about her answer that are not helpful to me, and that may be frustrating to both of you in the future."

Her husband sat down in his chair and leaned forward awaiting what I had to say. I could tell the neighbor's answer was not for him; but I guessed he didn't want to upset his wife further. So I said, "We do not yet know what caused your son's death but hopefully we will find out soon. That information may help other children—and their parents. And I'm sure as I can possibly be that God would never give you your precious son for those thirteen years and then suddenly take him back. I would never do such a thing in a million years, and I'm suggesting that God is far more loving than I am."

I asked the father if he would give a child to a family and then, without warning, take it back, and without hesitation, he said, "Rev. Fred, you know the answer to that."

Suddenly, his wife began to cry and said, "I'm so confused."

Her husband went to her side, and put his arm around her, and I continued, "I also believe that God is very concerned about your loss, and cares deeply about you at this moment, as I do. Now, we need to help you find the strength to face this situation, to make plans for the service of memory, and to find out what happened to your son so suddenly."

I put my arms around both of them, and we cried together, and they began to take hold of the work before them.

Actually, their son didn't feel well the morning of his death. He told both his parents that he didn't feel well. As I remember, his dad didn't take him too seriously, being a teacher and used to kids' efforts to miss school. It is conceivable that if dad had taken their son's complaint seriously, he would have called a doctor and possibly saved their son's life. We were never sure what happened.

Easy answers often do more harm than good, and keep us from searching for causes and solutions to human suffering.

Can't Please Them All

My father rarely gave advice. I believe he thought it was a "put down." On one occasion he said to me, "If you find anyone who has all the answers, run for your life."

Another time we were discussing professions, and he said, "Well, what about law, or medicine? You'd make a good doctor; and you're excellent in math."

I responded, my heartbeat quickening, "I think it is going to be the ministry."

He took another puff of his cigar, and a deep breath, and replied, "It is your choice, but you'll never earn any money, and you'll never please them."

"You'll never please them" is an interesting remark, because I so wanted to please my parishioners. In the ministry I learned quickly that what pleases one person, may displease another, and that trying to please everyone is a "dead end street."

I remember preaching a sermon entitled, "God Bless the Heretics." The first person who spoke to me after the service said, "Thanks for nothing."

The second person shook my hand warmly and said, "You were right on target this morning!"

When I returned from the march in Selma, Alabama, my mail was heavy for a few days. One man wrote, "Your cloth was erased. What I and many others saw was just another member of a mob, bent on destroying law and order in a little town over-run by hordes of semi-hysterical publicity seekers, ego-patters, and self-aggrandizers. I say, 'Long live Alabama and Governor Wallace, the last stand of American States Rights.' I sincerely hope you won't live to regret your past in these matters."

Re-reading these words after forty-one years is a painful reminder that you can't please them all. That letter expressed the sentiments of a number of people who wrote to me.

Another letter came to me the same day as the angry one. It was from Congressman James C. Corman of the House of Representatives, Congress of the United States.

Dear Fred, I have just read excerpts from the sermon you delivered upon your return from Selma, Alabama. I want to commend you and thank you for the active role you are taking in promoting interracial understanding and equal rights. You may be interested to know that the Judiciary Committee, of which I am a member, is completing hearings on the Voting Rights Bill. We hope to report the bill to the House within a few days and bring it to a vote before Easter. I am confident that the bill will receive overwhelming support in both the house and the Senate and will become law before this summer. In the final analysis, I think the success of civil rights legislation depends on individual Americans. When clergymen and other community leaders speak out strongly in favor fo equal rights, I believe our chances for success are all the greater. Thank you for helping to pick up where Congress must necessarily leave off.

This letter was representative of most people's feelings at least the ones I received.

So, to please others is not a worthy motive. They deserve your authenticity, your honest experience, and your courage. Only in this way may you call forth the best in them.

The Congregation Speaks

When I returned home from my civil rights march in Selma, Alabama, I reported my experiences to my congregation the following Sunday. At the close of the service, one man came up to me and said, "I was also in Selma, but I did not march with you and the others. I stood with my Southern brothers and sisters."

I was simply stunned to hear his remarks. His little daughter was one of my own daughter's best friends, but I had no idea he came from a Southern background.

After recovering from my surprise, I said. "I'm proud of you for your courage and for standing up for what your think is right. If you think what I said is unfair, you are welcome to address this congregation next Sunday morning and tell your side of the story."

He thought for a moment, and then said, "You're kidding!"

I called him by his first name and replied, "I've never been more serious."

He smiled and said, "Thanks for the offer." He decided not to accept it.

My response was not game playing. I made that kind of offer a number of times, because I felt that my parishioners needed to know that their thoughts and feelings and experience deserved expression and respect as much as mine. The result was a healthy give and take in board meetings and other gatherings, and the spirit was of openness and honesty.

Reading Scripture

One Sunday morning a man addressed me after the service with the comment, "Rev. Fred, I wish someone would teach you how to read scripture."

"Wow! I honestly can't remember my response, but I was surprised and quieted. I told a friend what the man had said and he replied, "He's right. Someone should teach you how to read scripture."

After college and seminary, and ten years in the ministry, now they tell me! The second man was a well-known Hollywood actor and I asked him if he would teach me and he smiled and said, "Of course. Set a time."

A few hours with a real pro, and everybody gained. It wasn't the first time I was enriched by what my congregation had to teach me!

Sanctuary

Last night I had trouble sleeping. I was thinking about sending my stories to the publisher this coming week, and I could relax for a while. But still, no sleep. Three memories emerged from my unconscious. One was about a woman, a social worker, who came early every Sunday morning, sitting quietly in her usual pew.

One morning, after the service, I asked her if she would mind telling me why she came to our church when she passed so many churches along the way from her home.

She responded immediately. "Well, it isn't because of your preaching, really. It has to do with the spirit of the place. You see, my work is a taxing one, and at the end of the day and the end of the week, I am weary and my body and my soul need restoration. To me, this place is, indeed, a place of renewal. I find stillness here, not the usual chatter. The flowers on the altar so carefully chosen, the candle light, sometimes the soft music from the organ are soothing. But most of all, it is the holy silence that restores me."

I kissed this woman on her forehead, and said, "Thank you," as tears filled my eyes and fell on my cheek.

Another new couple visited our church three or four Sundays in a row, and one Sunday, I ventured to ask them why they came, what they found here that brought them back.

The woman smiled and answered, "That's an easy one. Not one time have we been here that we didn't sense a concern for the people of the world. There is a genuine concern for others far beyond this congregation."

"We want to be a part of these concerns," the man beside her said as he shook my hand. Inside my palm was a $500 bill.

The third story that came to me was about the great soul Howard Thurman. He was the author of a number of books on spirituality and was a most successful minister of All People's Church in San Francisco. At the end of the service that morning, we were sitting in my office and he said to me, "When I first stepped into the narthex of this church, I thought, it is too new. There hasn't been enough time for the Spirit to hallow this place. But then, when I walked into the sanctuary, before the processional hymn, I knew old Howard (referring to himself) was wrong. The spirit is indeed in this place." He was quiet for a moment, and reading my facial response to his affirmation, he leaned over and smiled at me saying, "And don't you be so arrogant as to take credit for it." These three memories let me sleep, and I knew these stories—really one story—needed to be shared. It took years for that spirit to evolve.

Spirit of the living God, fall a fresh on me.

Civil Rights

Calling Dr. King

A few months after Dr. Martin Luther King Jr. spoke to my parish, a minister colleague from Los Angeles said to me, "You know, I'm a little angry that Dr. King came to speak to your congregation."

"How so?"

"Well, why didn't he come to one of our churches?"

"You mean, why didn't he come to your church for example?"

"Well, yes, or some other black church."

"I think I know the answer, but before I tell you let me ask you a question: Did you invite Dr. King to speak to your congregation?"

He had a sheepish grin and said, "No, as a matter of fact, I did not."

"You may have answered your own question but let me tell you a story."

So I told him the story. When I first discovered, Dr. King's book *Stride Toward Freedom, The Montgomery Bus Boycott Story*, I read it with reckless abandon. I resented any interruption until I had finished it. And guess what? I finished it on a Saturday night from my church office. Sounds strange doesn't it to be in the office on Saturday night when I had two services to conduct the next morning.

Well, stranger still, I couldn't contain myself until I tried to call Dr. King and thank him for the book and ask him to come to speak to my congregation.

All the reasons why it was foolish to call him didn't seem to occur to me. After getting his church number through long distance, I dialed the number. After the first ring, a voice answered: "Dr. King speaking."

I was dumbfounded and he spoke again before I responded.

I told him of my appreciation for the book and asked him if he would consider coming to California to speak to my congregation.

"Well, Rev. Doty as you might guess, I am a very busy man these days."

I interrupted him saying: "Dr. King, please do not tell me no. Tell me when. We can wait."

"Well, Brother Fred (not Rev. Doty) you are a very persuasive young minister. Why don't you call me a year from now and let's talk again."

"Thank you, thank you, you can bet on it."

A year later I called the church and Dr. King's secretary rang his office. He picked up the phone and said: "Brother Fred, it is you again." I could tell he was laughing. He continued: "You really do want me to come. Let's set a date and make our plan."

The minister hearing the story said, "I'm so glad he came, Brother Fred."

Martha and Dr. King

Martin Luther King Jr. has become a hero to millions of people in the United States and around the world. Wonderful stories abound of his life in all kinds of situations. As time passes, as with all heroes, the stories will get bigger and bigger, and in time, the line between the real and imaginary will become blurred.

There is a story that happened between Dr. King and my youngest daughter at our dinner table that already sounds like a tall tale, but is as true as the sky is blue, and it reveals qualities in Dr. King that one seldom hears.

My wife and I and our four daughters were having Sunday dinner and our guest was none other than Dr. Martin Luther King Jr. He had been the guest speaker at our Sunday morning service and was now our dinner guest.

As is our usual custom, we held hands around the table, asked for a blessing for our meal and our fellowship, and then began to pass the food. My youngest daughter Martha, age five, was not interested in food. We quickly learned that her agenda was Dr. King. She scooted down from her chair, ran around the table, and stroked Dr. King's face with her hand.

What on earth was going on? Martha now had center stage. I remember my embarrassment as though it all happened yesterday. Whatever her reason for stroking his face, she seemed satisfied and returned to her chair. Dr. King's amusement was revealed by his warm smile.

No sooner had Martha reached her seat, when she addressed Dr. King, "May I kiss you?"

Dr. King looked at me, saw my smile, and responded, "Kiss away, Martha!"

Martha ran around the table again, placed a resounding smack on Dr. King's cheek, and returned to her chair.

The rest of us began to eat our dinner, but Martha still had other things on her mind. Before she took a bite, she suddenly turned to Dr. King, saying,

"You're no doctor and you're no king. You don't have a satchel and you don't have a crown. You're just a plain old guy like my Dad."

We all laughed, but Dr. King's belly laugh drowned out the rest of us. Through his laughter, he finally said, "Oh, Martha, you are so right!"

Martha seemed content for a while, much to my relief, and we all proceeded to enjoy our dinner. After dessert was served and enjoyed, Martha entered the conversation once more, addressing Dr. King with a lilt in her voice. "Want to see my bedroom?"

I burst in, "Now, Martha, Dr. King is tired and . . ." I wasn't able to continue, because Dr. King interrupted, "Now, brother Fred, you leave Martha and me alone."

Martha immediately rushed to his side and they proceeded to see her bedroom, hand in hand. The rest of us sat, half in laughter and half in tears. Through the walls we could hear faint echoes of their voices, and all of a sudden another of Dr. King's belly laugh rang out and the words. "Oh, Martha, you are a card!"

A true story, a precious encounter between a mesmerized child and a great man who was fascinated by this uninhibited, forthright, angelic child.

Later, when we were alone, Dr. King said to me with a smile, "Your daughter reminds me of my son. They are about the same age, I'm guessing. I miss him."

Stay Where You Are

Dr. Martin Luther King and I were sitting together in my office. He had just preached to two overflowing crowds. I was deeply moved by his story of what was happening to his people in the South, and I wanted in some way to help the blacks in their struggle for justice and freedom.

He was quiet and his eyes were closed as if to be catching a "cat nap". When he opened his eyes, I said, "Dr. King, as you know, I was deeply moved by your book, *Stride Towards Freedom* and after this morning's sermon, I am considering coming to the South and hoping to become involved in the civil right's movement. Of course, I will have to discuss this with my wife and children. I love the people in this parish very much, but I am willing to come to the South if you think it is wise."

Dr. King did not hesitate a moment, but learned forward, placed his hand on my knee and said, "Brother Fred, stay where you are. I need you here!"

He hesitated a moment and then continued, "No other minister in a white, upper middle class parish has invited me to tell my story of segregation in the South."

He repeated the words, "I need you here" and then added, "And you will pay for inviting me. Yes, Brother Fred; you will pay!"

Wherever there are people, irrespective of their color, or religion, there is always a fight for freedom. And so, whoever you are, wherever you are, join the march for justice and freedom and sing the song, "We Shall Overcome!"

Begin, today, right where you are!

Old Negro Lady

We had gathered from all over the United States and Canada to march with Martin Luther King Jr. in Selma. His call had come after "Bloody Sunday" when Sheriff Jim Clark and his men on foot and on horseback beat defenseless American citizens. Sheriff Jim Clark's voice could be heard clearly in the background, "Get those goddamned niggers and get those goddamned white niggers."

The troopers were under Governor George C. Wallace's orders to stop the Negroes walk for freedom from Selma to Montgomery. They chased the screaming, bleeding marchers nearly a mile back to their church, clubbing them as they ran.

Ambulances screamed in relays between Good Samaritan Hospital to Brown's Chapel Church carrying hysterical men women, and children suffering head wounds and tear gas burns. (Quotes from John Lewis, *Walking With the Wind*). Much of this nightmare was mirrored on national television and King sent out a call for help and I was one of many who responded.

Many of us slept the first night on the ground in an open field. There was excitement everywhere and uncertainty about what might happen the next day, the day of the march.

Sleeping next to me was an old Negro lady who had walked from sunup to sundown "to be a part of the march."

"Where you from?" she asked

"I'm from the Los Angeles area of California."

"That's a fur piece, ain't it?"

"Yes ma'am, that really is a 'fur piece'. "

She cackled and said, "No white person in this area ever called ma'am, not in my whole life. She continued, "I gets myself up fo' daylight and I walk until near the sun goes down, but I ain't too tired cause I's marching for freedom." (Her face! I wish to God you could have seen it —like she's ready to enter the promised land.)

"We sho' is grateful to have you come all this way to help us in our march for freedom."

"I consider it a high privilege to walk beside you. You been waiting a long time for your freedom and you deserve it."

"You look like you hongry," she said and continued, "Would you like an aig (egg) sandwich? I'z got a whole sack full."

"You bet I would. I haven't had an egg sandwich in a long time."

So we talked and ate egg sandwiches until we dropped off to sleep. What a gift to have this precious time with that lady, and I didn't even get her name or phone number (which she probably didn't have). It was worth coming a "fur piece" to be able to walk with that rare soul to get some idea of what they were willing to pay for freedom.

I Knows My Place

In the spring of 2003 I heard Dr. Joseph Lowery speak at the Martin Luther King Center in Atlanta. Dr. Lowery worked with Dr. King all during the Civil Rights area and was a member of the Southern Christian Leadership Conference, and for a time the president of the SCLC. Near the end of his speech he told a simple story that I shall remember for a long time, a story that Dr. King may have known and treasured.

An old two-car train trudged along near Tuskegee, Alabama, on its journey to Birmingham. It was pouring down rain and one of the two cars was leaking like a sieve. This was the car for "black folks." The other car was for "white folks", and it was high and dry.

An old black man and his wife were standing on the little porch (just outside the door) getting soaking wet. A few feet away on the little porch of the other car was an old white man and his wife and they were quite dry.

The white man said to the black man, "Why don't you and your wife come on over here where it is dry?"

"Oh, no," the black man replied, "Thank you sir, but we knows our place."

The white man waited a moment and then replied, "It isn't good for us to be here where it is dry while the two of you are standing there in the rain."

I don't remember everything Dr. Lowery said that day, but I remember that story and I remember it well. It spoke to a feeling and a connection I had even as a child. It's not (good for me to drink at a fountain for whites and you to drink at a fountain for blacks; it is not good for me to attend a school with the best in every way and you to have to go to second class schools; it's not good for me to live in a nice home and for you to live in a shack that has no toilet or running water, it is not good for me to have a community pool to swim in and for you to read a sign saying, "For Whites Only." It is not good for me; it is not good for my country; it is not good for my world; it is not good for my soul.

We Don't Want You Here!

The first Selma march was greeted with the use of violence on the part of the police. People were beaten with Billy clubs from mounted police, as they were tear gassed and then beaten as they hurried to escape. The horrible sight was photographed and presented to the world on television and by newspapers. Martin Luther King Jr. sent out a plea for help and thousands of people came to Selma to join in a second march intended to go from Selma to Montgomery. And I was one of them.

I was still living in southern California and even though King had urged me to "stay where you are," I knew this was a crisis and I had to respond to his plea. While we were walking around waiting for the march to begin, an attractive young woman, well dressed as if going to the office, walked up to me and said, "We do not want you here; we do not think you belong here; we think we can solve our own problems."

She hesitated and then continued, "But God must want you here or you wouldn't be here."

This woman was not mean. I did not see hate in her eyes or sense it in her muscles. I felt her sincerity and I admired her courage. And I definitely shared her pain. I said to her, "I'm sorry that you are hurting. I can well understand that you do not want us here. My dear parents are southern born and bred and they do not want us here. And if I did not feel that God wants me here, I wouldn't be here."

She looked me straight in the eye and turned and walked away. I hurt deep inside. I think we shared a moment of pain together.

"Nigger Lover"

The phone rang in the middle of the night. I woke easily because I had not been sleeping soundly. These phone calls at 2:00 and 3:00 and 4:00 in the morning had started after my march on Selma with Dr. Martin Luther King Jr. These calls usually contained angry voices often screaming obscenities like "You god damn nigger lover." But this night, the voice was more sinister and the words, "Rev. Doty, you have four little girls, don't you and they come home from school at such and such an hour" sent a cold chill through my whole body. I was momentarily speechless and when I tried to speak, I gasped and my voice cracked.

When I did speak, I was able to say essentially the following words: "Yes, I do have four wonderful little girls, Mary, Molly, Margaret and Martha. They are God's gift to my wife and me. We love them very much, but you likely know that, especially if God has blessed you and your wife with your own children. I wish you well as you attempt to be good parents and to model before them the life you want them to live. And I congratulate you on your trying to carry out the strength of your conviction by calling me at this strange hour."

I waited and waited and there was only a quiet click on the other end of the line.

O God, I have such mixed feelings of those years. I am grateful for the privilege of being able to know a lot of wonderful, simple folk who risked their lives day after day in their search for freedom and dignity. I was humbled again and again by their amazing courage in the presence of unbridled hate. I am grateful for those rare moments when a sense of Thy presence stilled the fearful coward in me and enabled me to join with them in attempting to witness for what we believed to be right and true; and may I never forget those brothers and sisters who gave their lives in an attempt to find a better way. May I continue the search for them and for me in our attempt to create a world where all men and women are truly free. And somehow help me to understand the fear and loneliness of those who call at 3:00 in the morning. Amen.

Unheralded Heroes

I am often invited to speak to high school and college youth about my experiences in the civil rights years. Many of the youth have read or skimmed King's first book, *Stride Toward Freedom*, the chronicle of 50,000 Negroes who took to heart the principle of non-violence during the Montgomery, Alabama bus boycott. I am especially interested in the questions that the young people ask when my presentation is finished.

One of the questions that often gets asked is, "Who is the white man sitting beside Dr. King in the first non-segregated bus ride down the streets of Montgomery."

The students seemed to be surprised that King would invite a white man to be his bus partner on that historic occasion. Why not Rosa Parks or Rev. Ralph Abernathy or Andrew Young or some other black person, who had been a vital part of the movement?

I am always pleased when someone asks that question, because I believe Rev. Glenn Smiley is one of the unsung heroes of the Civil Rights Movement and a great soul in so many ways.

Glenn was a close friend of my second wife, Kathy, and her husband Hugh Beaumont, and during those turbulent years shared his experiences in the Movement when he visited them in Southern California; and kept in contact with them with regular correspondence.

Glenn was Field Secretary for the F.O.R.—the Fellowship of Reconciliation, the renowned organization dedicated to and experienced in the techniques of non-violence when confronting divisive situations that so often, in human experience, led to brutality and even death.

Glenn Smiley was the natural person to send when the Montgomery Improvement Association needed help in teaching its people the techniques (and necessary attitudes) of non-violent confrontation, proposed and used by Gandhi of India.

Glenn had been imprisoned for pacifist resistance to military service in World War II. He was a "mild-mannered" white Methodist minister from Texas, who looked like one, until he spoke on the subject of race, civil rights and non-violence (from Taylor Branch, *Parting the Waters*). Interestingly enough, Taylor Branch reports that the first advice Glenn gave to Dr. King was "get rid of the guns around the house."

Having lived in the South, Glenn was well aware of the deep, painful injustices of segregation in that part of the country, and once wrote to Kathy and Hugh, "What the South needs to help solve the seemingly impossible problems of segregation is a Savior." My guess is that he probably had been thinking of someone like Mahatma Gandhi.

Shortly afterwards, another letter from Glenn arrived with this news, "I think we have found a savior; but he is not white, he is black." He was referring, of course, to Dr. Martin Luther King Jr.

Rev. Robert Graetz, the only white minister of a Negro church in Montgomery, said of Smiley, "few people realized the role that Glenn Smiley and Bayard Rustin played in the Montgomery protest."

Both men carefully avoided the limelight. Although Glenn had many close contacts with Dr. King, he rarely talked about what they had discussed, or mentioned the influence he may have had on King.

Glenn Smiley, and other Fellowship of Reconciliation leaders, were readily available for their services to the Montgomery Blacks. Mass meetings became training sessions in the techniques of non-violence. In these sessions participants engaged in role-playing, taking the parts of bus drivers, white and black passengers, police officers, all acting out various scenarios involving physical and verbal abuse. In this way, Glenn and other F.O.R. leaders taught the negroes of Montgomery, a few at a time, how to put the non-violent philosophy into practice.

Glenn told us that he was amazed at how quickly the Blacks responded to the role playing, and how creative they were in their responses.

He shared with us a story of a black woman who stepped on to the segregated bus, and stopped before the only empty seat available, The empty seat was filled with packages, obviously belonging to a white woman who was holding her head stiffly as she gazed out the window. The black woman stood there, puzzled, uncertain what to do. Then, she managed a smile and said, "Excuse me, Ma'am, but may I hold your packages as we ride along together?"

There is no doubt in my mind that those black men and women deeply appreciated and loved Glenn Smiley for his skills in non-violent responses to violence provoking situations.

Very little is written about Smiley in the Civil Rights books and much of that had to do with Glenn himself. He wanted as little publicity as possible. After all, he knew, this was a movement that grew out of the desperation of the Blacks themselves, and it was they who began the long, painful "Stride Toward Freedom." But for those who knew him personally, he will remain a beacon to us who are still concerned about issues of justice and equality among all of the citizens of our country.

Glenn Smiley was a great soul, and the fact that Dr. King chose him to ride beside him in the first non-segregated bus ride, "tells a mint."

Rev. Charles Billups in Birmingham

Charles Billups is an obscure Baptist minister in Birmingham, Alabama. Having a wife and six children to support he has an additional job in a factory. One midnight, in the spring of 1959, as he was leaving for home, eight hooded men seized him, shoved him in a car and drove to a clearing in the woods. There they stripped him naked, roped him around a tree and beat him with a chain. These Klansmen had been drinking and they were angry. What especially infuriated them was this black man's too effective efforts in the local Martin Luther King program for human rights; his stubborn integrity also upset them. Determined to make him cringe and use their word "nigger," they kept beating him with the chain. He stood his ground. Frustrated, they announced he would have to die. But first he might have something to say? He did. This, roughly, is what it was:

"Father, forgive these men. May their children not have to carry the guilt of what they are doing. And may they get an education. May my children also get an education, a better one than I did. Nevertheless, not what I will but what You will. For Jesus' sake. Amen."

Before daylight Billups was thrown into a ditch beside a highway. Two policemen in a patrol car later picked him up and left him in a hospital. It took doctors more than an hour to clean the dirt out of the gashes on his back and legs. The first night home an armed bodyguard of friends kept watch. Next night Billups asked them all to go to their homes. Although he had been afraid the night before, he wasn't anymore. There was no need of weapons; it was enough to trust in God.

One of Billups's friends, Rev. Glenn Smiley, interviewed him three years later. Smiley had heard the story but he wanted to be sure of the details. When Billups was through double-checking them he smiled and said, "You know, a funny thing happened right here in this house less than a month ago. You're the first white person I've told it to. It was very late at night. Some one was at the door knocking. I let the man in. He looked nervous and unhappy. Then he said, "I'm one of the eight men who nearly beat you to death three years ago. My conscience won't let me go on in this way. I can't stand it. I want to be forgiven. I'll go to the police if you like and give them my name and the names of the other seven men.'"

"No," I said, "I don't want you to do that. I'm guilty too. Let's kneel down and ask God to forgive us both."

This incredible story was told to my wife by her dear friend.

Black Youth in Camp

Three scenes continue to cross my mind from time to time, three scenes from the incredible 1960s—three scenes touching upon the turmoil, the pain, the frustration, the anger, the creativity, even the love of the 60s. A group of upper middle class white youth is in the slum areas of Pacoima, California sanding and caulking and painting and singing and laughing.

Side by side are the poor blacks and Chicanos who are laughing and singing as they see the rooms of the dirty old ramshackled building transformed into a recreation center. They will have a place of their own to talk and play and to dance and to sing. I remember so well the paint on the walls, on their clothes, even on their faces, put there purposefully as psychological walls broke down as the kids worked together in that meaningful project.

A second scene I witnessed on television as did millions of other

Americans. We were dumbfounded as we watched Watts in Los Angeles, California, being burned and looted and raped, mainly by angry, frustrated, bewildered blacks. Before our eyes, police cars were attacked, buildings were burned, businesses were robbed, and firefighters stood by helplessly while angry mobs kept the fires burning. This spectacle of horror went on into the night.

A third scene took place not far from Pacoima and Watts not long after the Watts riots. A group of youth, Negroes, Chicanos, Chinese, Whites, mixtures of blood, all together at a campsite in the hills, living together for a few days. They were working together, eating together, worshipping together, dancing together and now they are crying together—crying because they are at their final campfire before returning to their homes again. A tall, athletic black teenager stands up and tries to speak the message of his heart.

The kids in the circle are at rapt attention for this young man has won their respect and their admiration and their love. He's simply terrific, strong, bright, musical, great dancer, great guy. He says in broken words, amidst his tears, "I will never forget you, never. These last few days have been heaven for me, and I don't want this night to end. All my life I have heard the words 'hate whites' but now I know I can never hate a white person as long as I live."

He started to return to his seat by the fire and he was mobbed by youth and counselors alike, ending in a circle of love and the haunting words began again, "We shall overcome; we shall overcome some day; deep in my heart, I do believe; we shall overcome some day."

Cool, Man

I like stories about children and I like to tell stories about children. There is something disarming and delightful about their honesty. They so often share exactly what they feel, no "sugar coating" just what they feel.

One of my sister's grandsons is such a child. He is energetic, clever, very bright and into life with gusto. His energy level is off the map and it is a delight to be around him. Recently, he was scheduled to spend the weekend with his grandparents. A day or two before he was to come he called and asked his grandmother if he could bring his friend with him for the weekend. For a number of reasons it was not convenient and she suggested another time would be better for her.

Disappointed with her remarks, he broke in with the words, "But grandmother, he is my best friend and he won't be any trouble."

His tone of voice and the way grandmothers feel about their grandchildren changed the tide and she said, "Ah, well, I guess it will be alright."

When the two children arrived the grandparents were ready and waiting for them. The best friend turned out to be a little black boy which was quite a surprise for the grandparents. This was a small town in Tennessee and the first time a black person had ever been an overnight guest with the grandparents. Why didn't Jake tell the grandparents his best friend was black? Because he was a child and it never occurred to him. He was color-blind, thank God; and it was a great weekend for everyone.

One of Jake's aunts and uncles had invited a black teenager to live with them. His aunt was the boy's teacher, and she learned he was having a tough time at home and might have to drop out of school. She really cared about the young man and cared about his future. She talked it over with her husband, and they agreed to invite the young man to live with them and finish his schooling. It turned out to be a blessing for everyone.

One weekend Jake and his grandparents were visiting with his aunt and uncle and their new son. Jake latched on to the new teenager and they began to shoot some baskets with Jake's ever present basketball. All of a sudden Jake said to his new friend, "Aren't we kind of cousins or something?"

The young man explained how he had been invited to join Jake's aunt and uncle's family and Jake simply replied, "Cool." Now on with the game. Cool indeed!

KKK

I attended a conference a few years ago in Virginia and met a man who was one of the leaders of my small group. I commented on how much I appreciated his leadership. One thing led to another, and I happened to mention that I was interested in the civil rights movement. He surprised me by commenting that he had been a member of the Ku Klux Klan for a number of years. I had noticed that he easily related to blacks at the conference, so I asked him what had changed his attitude.

He said it was really quite simple. His wife was a nurse at the Duke University Hospital and a number of her colleagues in the nursing department were blacks. He was invited to a dinner where he was seated by the husband of one of the black nurses. At first it was quite awkward, but the man turned out to be a warm, gentle, and interesting person. He discovered that he had a number of interests in common with this black man and before the evening was over, he was a changed man.

Dr. Martin Luther King, Jr., said on a number of occasions that the white man doesn't like us because he doesn't know us; and he felt that when he got to know the negroes he would discover that he had more in common with them than he had differences.

I grew up in Old Hickory, Tennessee, a segregated mill town. Negroes lived in separate parts of town. We would see them in the grocery store and occasionally a Negro woman would help my mother with the washing and ironing, but we had almost no personal contact with blacks. Everything was separated and the attitude was clearly that blacks were an inferior people. The few blacks I got to know were black women and without exception I found them to be capable, kind and easy to relate to. In no way did the word inferior apply, and early on I knew deep down that segregation was wrong.

In seminary I met people from all over the world and blacks, browns, yellows, and all shades in between were delightful, and I was greatly enriched by the experience. Early in my ministry I invited people from other races to speak, to lead seminars, and to share in many ways with our congregation. And Dr. King was right, when we got to know them we got to appreciate them and to love them. They enriched our lives and we shall be forever blessed because of them.

Fist Fight

A number of times as a minister I have been challenged to a fist fight, the last thing I could have imagined when I decided to become a minister. I learned early, however, that people can easily become upset and even enraged over something you say or do or stand for. It often happens over personal issues or controversial issues like civil rights or abortion. As we all know from the ever present media, people are attacked and even murdered over issues that profoundly threaten one's position.

I received threatening phone calls all hours of the day and night when I marched with Martin Luther King, Jr. in Selma, Alabama after the horrible results of "Bloody Sunday" when men, women and children were attacked by hate filled policeman on horses wielding billy clubs on their heads and bodies.

At least four times I was challenged to a fist fight when men became upset with me over one issue or another. Interestingly enough all four backed down when I accepted the challenge. I learned nothing in college or seminary to prepare me for those moments. By that comment, I am suggesting that there could have been and should have been.

One of the reasons why Martin Luther King's non-violent marches were so successful was that he was abundantly clear about the philosophy of the nonviolent movement and the practical techniques that were necessary in violent situations. Countless hours were spent with men like Glenn Smiley from the Fellowship of Reconciliation saturating people with the philosophy of nonviolence. Dr. King himself spent many hours pouring over the writings of the great Indian leader Mahatma Gandhi in the attempt to understand his philosophy of nonviolence and to learn specific techniques to use when confronted with angry and violent attackers.

Millions of Americans have heard over and over again the soul moving words of Dr. King "Violence begets the very thing it seeks to destroy, adding deeper darkness to a night already devoid of stars. Darkness cannot drive out hate. Only love can do that."

The first thing that Dr. King said to those of us who marched in Selma was, "If you are here out of anger for our white brothers, do not march. If you feel you cannot be beaten and not turn the other cheek, do not march. If you feel that you cannot be nonviolent in any situation you may encounter, do not march. For you see, we must return love for hate. We must show our angry white brothers that we love them. Violence cannot drive out hate. Only love can do that."

I wish I had been confronted by that kind of wisdom earlier in my life. Surely I had heard the words of Jesus, "He who fights by the sword shall die by the sword," but that's a far cry from the program that King used with his followers.

Affirmative Action

I attended an interracial conference in Los Angeles. Hundreds of clergy were present from all over southern California. We were discussing the issue of Affirmative Action. I stood up, was recognized by the chairperson, and said, "I am opposed to the idea of Affirmative Action." Before I could explain why I was against the idea, the chairperson interrupted me saying, "I can't believe my ears. Not you, Fred Doty. I thought you were our friend.

A bit surprised at his quick response. I said, "You thought right. I am your friend, and I will continue to be your friend. Whether you are my friend or not depends on you. I assumed that our friendship does not depend upon our agreeing on every issue; in fact, just the opposite. You see, I feel in some ways this issue is a put down to my black brothers and sisters. It assumes they can't compete on an equal basis with whites and need special privileges."

Before I could say anything more, he smiled and replied, "Thank you, Brother Fred, for your kind words and forgive me for doubting you, even for a moment."

A gentle laughter from the audience followed and the meeting continued. When it was over, the U.S. Congressman from the area walked up to me and said, "Good afternoon, Fred. Thanks for your statement about Affirmative Action. I wanted to make the same statement; but it would not help me to do so in this audience." We both laughed.

In the last few years, I have changed my mind on that issue. I am now for Affirmative Action. And that is another story.

Watts

In the summer of 1965 the Watts riots occurred, and Los Angeles was a nightmare for a few days with rioting and burning and killing. Governor Pat Brown was called home from a vacation in Greece and mobilized 14,000 National Guards to help the police attempt to bring order. Watts dominated the news for most of the week, and millions watched on TV in amazement and horror. Leaders like Mayor Yorty and Governor Brown and others traded jibes over who was responsible.

Much talk was made of Martin Luther King, Jr., going to Watts to try and calm the rioters, though Governor Brown and Mayor Yorty did not want King in L.A. Later, King did go to Watts, where he was jeered and told to go home with his nonviolent approach. He slowly calmed the crowd, listened to their grievances, and offered hope for a new day.

Later King reported that there were more people killed in Watts in a few days than in the whole civil rights movement up to that time. There was no way to be sure about such statistics, because many civil rights deaths were never known about in the backwoods and towns of Mississippi and other Southern states.

I lived one hour from Watts, and watched in dismay and pain, and wondered what my congregation could do to help the leaders in Watts find some hope in what appeared to be a hopeless situation. Shortly after the rioting stopped and order was restored, I investigated who the leaders in Watts were, and called Walter Bremond, the chairperson of the Brotherhood Crusade. Bremond and Ron Karenga were the names given me as key leaders in Watts.

I called Mr. Bremond and told him that I would like to meet with him and evaluate the possibility of our laymen working with his board to address some of the problems they were facing. He laughed and replied sarcastically: "Oh, you would like to help us with our concerns, would you, Rev. Doty? Well—let me tell you how you can do that. You get an executive from IBM, Litton Industries, the National Association of Manufacturers, General Electric, a vice president from USC or UCLA, perhaps Sidney Poitier—and then call me and we'll meet with you."

I responded, "Mr. Bremond, set the date for our first meeting."

Bremond quickly replied, "I guess you didn't hear me, Rev. Doty."

"Yes, I heard you, and I will have most of those people present. I will need some time to have them check their schedules." What Mr. Bremond did not know was that all these people were in my parish, except for Sydney Poitier.

He was quiet for a moment, then said, "You are serious, aren't you?"

"I've never been more serious in my life."

The dates were set, and for almost three years, we alternated monthly meetings on Saturday mornings in Watts and Woodland Hills in the San Fernando Valley. These meetings were real eye openers for both groups, and we learned to listen to each other and to cooperate in enabling the leaders in Watts to achieve certain goals for their people.

Specific concerns had to do with supermarkets, service stations, banks, training for leadership, and other areas. We were able to relate on practical issues, to be serious at the highest levels, to cement some friendships, to laugh together and to achieve some goals for the Watts group.

Walter Bremond became a real friend, and we met occasionally after the group broke up. I'll never forget a call I received one day when Walter said, "I miss my friend, let's get together." That was a high day in my ministry; because I, too, had missed my friend.

We had some good laughs to temper the serious. As we gathered one morning, just before the meeting began, one of the black men turned to the head of Litton Industries and said, "Hey, man, how many cats you got working for you?"

"Well," he responded with a grin, "Quite a lot."

"Ah, come on, how many?"

"To be exact, 10,001."

"Ten thousand, you say ten thousand? That's a lot of cats, man" and with a gesture and laughter he raised his right palm and slapped the Litton Manager's hand with affection. It was a fun moment for all and a great way to begin a meeting.

Rural Hospital

Disagreement

I was only a few days into a new job, and one person had been particularly kind in helping me to get established. He was the supervisor for another agency with whom I would be working regularly. There was a strong likelihood that I would be called on to lead some training sessions for members of his staff. One Friday night he and his wife invited my wife and me for an evening meal. It was an excellent meal and we were having a fun evening getting acquainted. When we had finished our dessert, our wives suggested that they would "do the dishes" while the two men talked business.

After a bit of idle chatter, my host began to discuss his personnel philosophy, and he added that he assumed I felt the same way. As gently as I could, I said that I came at it in a little different way. Before I could finish my thought, he said, "You're really saying you don't agree with me. I can't believe you. You're a guest in my home and you disagree with my ideas?"

I was taken aback, to say the least. I finally managed to say, "I'm sorry I've upset you. You've been so kind to us these days, and both Kathy and I are most appreciative. At the same time, in a way, I'm glad this misunderstanding has occurred, because it would come up sooner or later. You asked me a question and I gave you an honest answer. I assumed you wanted just that. I could have been cautious and tried to say just what you wanted me to say. In doing that I would have assumed that you weren't interested in my honest answer, but only to mirror your opinion. I choose not to tiptoe around you, but to be open and honest with you and do the same with our staff relations."

About that time, our wives appeared from the kitchen and Kathy reminded me that we needed to go. We thanked our hosts and left.

The next morning my secretary came into my office and said, "Mr. —— is here and wonders if you would have a sack lunch with him today."

"Send him in."

He was a tall man and a strong man. With a smile on his face, he reached out and hugged me and said, "I don't want you to tip-toe around me. I want us to have an open relationship."

He had prepared a sack lunch and we went to the local park, the beginning of a growing and meaningful relationship. So many relationships never develop out of fear, and much is lost.

Courtroom

I was on the stand in the courtroom being questioned by a lawyer. I was very frustrated, because the lawyer seemed determined to have a question answered "yes" or "no." Rather than permit me to clarify the situation as I understood it, I started to speak and the lawyer would break in with, "Please, Rev. Doty, answer the question, 'yes' or 'no'."

I sat silent for a few moments to clarify my frustration and hesitation when the judge spoke to me, "Reverend Doty, do you understand the question?"

Suddenly, the sky was clear for me, and I said, "Judge, do you want me to answer the question, or do you want the truth?"

The lawyer appeared dumbfounded; the judge seemed to be perplexed, and had a slight grin on his face. He announced that there would be a short recess, and there was a trickle of laughter in the courtroom. The judge and lawyer huddled together for a private conversation. Shortly, the judge called the court to order, and he said, "Reverend Doty. We would like the truth." His face seemed to express amusement rather than frustration or hostility. Much relieved, I clarified my position and the case continued.

Many times in my ministry, I have had cause to remember that courtroom experience. In the midst of an argument with another person that seemed to be going nowhere, I have a flashback, and the question appears. "Do you want to win an argument, or are you desirous of hearing the other person's position?" If I truly hear that other person out, he will know it, and that may well be the ice breaker for reconciliation.

Imaging And Healing

During my employment as a mental health consultant at the rural hospital, I went to a conference on *Imaging As An Aid To Healing*. Most of our leaders were medical doctors, and clergy persons, all from medical settings. One of the presenters was a professor at Marquette University and he related the following story:

A young intern was sitting in a doctor's lounge after lunch, drinking a cup of coffee. Nearby, well within hearing range, were three or four doctors, discussing a certain male patient. This man was losing weight, refused to eat, and felt he was going to die. All medical procedures revealed nothing that would cause this man to be in this condition. The intern had become extremely interested in the convention, and needed to visit the young man who thought he was going to die.

In the late afternoon, when most doctors had gone home and things were quieted down, the intern went into this patient's room. He introduced himself and related to the patient the conversation that he had heard from the doctors. And he added, "I think you know what the problem is, and I am most interested. I wonder if you would tell me what is happening."

Without hesitation the patient said, "It's quite simple. I've been hexed and I'm going to die. A medicine man put a hex on me, and there's nothing anyone can do to change that."

The intern said, "That's what I thought. You see, I was once hexed myself, and I thought sure I was going to die, but I got unhexed."

The patient raised up, leaned forward and stared in disbelief. The intern continued, "I can unhex you, but no one must know, and you must do exactly as I tell you."

The intern looked around to be sure no one could hear the conversation. The patient listened intently. The intern leaned forward and whispered, "I will come for you at 1 A.M. exactly. All will be asleep. We will go to this special room, and I will show you what to do."

The patient, wide-eyed, readily agreed.

At exactly one o'clock, this intern appeared, had the patient put on his robe, and together they walked to a quiet room. The room was darkened, except for a small table covered by a dark cloth which was covered with many candles. One candle was lighted, and the intern asked the patient to light the other candles as he read some "magic" words (gibberish). Then, with closed eyes he stood behind the patient and asked him to listen carefully as he pricked the patient's skin and ordered the evil spirits to leave this man's body. He then clapped his hands loudly, and ordered the spirits to leave. He then asked the patient to blow out the lights, and the hex would be over.

He then said, "You are unhexed. No one must know. I want you to join me in the doctor's dining room for breakfast as a celebration."

The patient was ecstatic, and readily agreed to the celebration breakfast.

The next morning the doctors were dumbfounded at the patient eating, and relating to the intern, who later shared his experiences with the "man who had been hexed."

I've learned through the years the power of the mind-set, and its incredible ability, despite technical knowledge, to control life and death. I have never used "hexing"—or unhexing myself, but am most respectful of the mind's power to influence and even control our destiny.

Stroke Patient

I have a friend, one I had known since childhood, who was a few months away from retirement. She was excited about her future, and the realization of her many dreams. A few months before her retirement date, she suffered a major stroke. She was paralyzed on her left side and learned soon that she would never work again, or drive again. She learned also, that she would have to get most of her nourishment from a tube.

I visited her many times in a nursing home, and I listened to her express her bewilderment, welcomed her anger, and wiped her tears.

One morning I shall never forget. Shortly after I arrived, an old black lady came into her room carrying a bucket, a mop, and cleaning supplies. After greeting my friend, she cleaned the room very carefully, from floor to ceiling. When she had finished, she turned to my friend and said, "Have a nice day, Miss Jean."

Jean did not respond. Shortly, a nurse entered the room and started to pull the drapes to let in the morning light. Jean spoke to the nurse, testily, "I didn't ask you to pull the drapes!"

The nurse, a little surprised, responded, "I just thought maybe—but before she could finish, Jean broke in, "When I want the drapes open, I'll tell you."

The nurse quietly left the room.

In another minute or two, there was a gentle knock on the door, and I opened it. There were two young women with smiling faces who had come to do physical therapy with Jean. I invited them in, and one of them cheerfully responded, "We're here to do your physical therapy."

Jean replied, curtly, "I do not want physical therapy!"

"But it will help you."

Cutting the therapist off abruptly, Jean repeated in a stern tone, "I do not want physical therapy!"

The young women turned to leave, and one said, "Perhaps tomorrow."

There was stone silence when the therapists left. Minutes passed, and I finally said, "Jean, I know you are angry, and you have a right to be angry. Dreams shattered, hopes lost, options limited."

Silence.

After a few moments, I continued, "From my perspective, God visited this room three times this morning. First, in the person of a dear old black woman who cleaned your room with all the loving care that your beloved mother would have done, and she left with a gentle greeting. You uttered not a word.

"The second time, God appeared in the person of a nurse who started to open the drapes and bring the morning light into your room. You dismissed her abruptly and harshly.

"The third time God entered your room in the person of two lovely young therapists who sought to massage your tired body and to bring new life to your muscles. You scolded them and sent them away. You did these things out of choice, and I support you in your right to make that choice. Much as I feel your pain and understand your anger, I believe you have other choices. I'm going to take a walk and I want you to decide if this is the way you want to respond to your pain, or if there is another way you wish to live your life."

Nothing more was said, and I slowly left the room. I returned in half an hour, sat down and immediately Jean said, still angry, "I want my physical therapists to return, and I want them right now."

"I will ask the head nurse if the physical therapists can fit you into their schedule. I imagine they have a lot of patients who wish to see them."

I went out to the main desk, and one of the therapists was writing on a patient's chart. I related to her what had happened, and her eyes filled with tears. She responded, "Thank you so much for believing in us. We'll do our very best with her. She can expect us shortly after lunch."

I do not know what happened after lunch, but it must have been a meaningful experience for Jean. She apparently did a lot of serious thinking and praying the next few weeks. I had to leave Jean shortly before lunch in order to catch a plane. When I hugged her goodbye, her eyes were wet and she clung to me before letting me go.

Months later, I visited her again. We had just begun to visit when her nurse appeared to do her work and I stepped out into the hall. Soon the nurse came out, and she said to me, "Your friend is the most caring patient I have. She always asks about my children, and calls them by name. She treats me like I'm somebody, and makes my day."

I returned to Jean's room, and she immediately began to tell me how wonderful her caretakers and nurses were. She asked me to help her into her wheelchair, because she wanted me to meet some people. We rolled down the hall. She seemed to appreciate each person we met and she seemed especially interested in my meeting the occupational therapist. She was a beautiful, alive, and kind woman, and very appreciative of Jean. We discussed the therapist's plans to attend graduate school, and it was a fun visit.

When we were back in Jean's room, she remarked, concerning the young therapist, "Isn't she an angel?" On my way out of the nursing home, I passed the therapist's office. She waved to me, thanked me for coming and said, "Isn't Jean an angel!"

I smiled and said, "That's what she said about you, and I agree with her."

The "angel" responded with a warm hug and light in her eyes and said, "Come again real soon!"

Sex Education

In the last few years of my ministry when I served as mental health consultant in a Catholic hospital, part of my work was to help meet the mental health needs of the community. I worked with doctors and teachers in this endeavor.

On one occasion, our medical chief of staff, the high school principal and I arranged for some community meetings at the hospital to help parents understand and help their kids with their concerns about sex education. For the first meeting, there was a huge turnout, much to our delight, affirming our suspicion that parents would welcome such an opportunity.

As soon as I welcomed the people, I started to introduce our leaders when a minister sitting in the back of the room asked to be recognized, and he rose and said, "There are some of us ministers who have come tonight to protest this meeting. We feel that it is not the role of the school or the hospital to teach our kids sexual education. We feel this should be done in the home by Christian parents."

I thanked the minister for coming and said, "I certainly can't disagree with having concerned and enlightened parents involved in their children's education concerning sex. May I call for a raising of hands of all those here who feel they are doing a good job of sexual education for their children. Will you please close your eyes and the doctor and principal will help me count the hands.

I waited. We all waited, and no hands were raised, not a single one. I then said, "Thank you, ministers, for helping to clarify the situation. Since there is no one present who feels that he is doing a good job of teaching sex education to his/her children, perhaps we can help with that. And we will be pleased to have any of you share your insights and experiences in this endeavor."

There was a lot of give and take after that, lots of questions, some heartfelt sharing and warm humor. At the end, people expressed a desire to continue the sessions. None of the ministers said a word. Several came to each session, and even began to ask questions. That was a definite positive.

Self-hate

During that time at the hospital, a woman came to me asking for my help with a personal problem. Her self-hate was so powerful that it was destroying her relationship with her children and her husband. She spent many hours of the day in her bedroom with the shades down. She came out when the children came home from school, because she wanted to be with them, and share what was going on at school; and then, often went back to bed.

She knew that her hermit-like existence was not good for her or her family, but she seemed helpless to alter the pattern. She had once been a nurse, and she enjoyed it; but she resigned from the hospital for personal reasons.

Her self-hate came from some things she had done as a young woman for which she felt God could not forgive her. From my perspective, her so-called sins were most understandable, certainly not severe enough to separate her from the love of God.

I worked with her individually, and in a small group of women. She attended faithfully and was much loved by the members of the group. Though the group was very meaningful to her, its benefits never seemed to pierce her shell of self-hate. As might be expected, as others shared their secrets, she was the most understanding and compassionate.

As the years months and years passed, she pulled up the shades in her living room, and ventured more into her yard and into the community, but I never felt we were able to help her lift her out of the vale of self-hate.

On one occasion, I asked her if she felt I loved her, and if she felt that in any way I blamed her, and she said, "No, I know for sure that you love me, and that you accept me for what I am."

I said, "I'm so glad because you are one of the most lovable persons I have ever met." I said further, "But your God doesn't love you; His love isn't as big as my love. Your God is too small and vindictive. He is not the God of Jesus Christ who forgives you and loves you dearly."

She hesitated for a moment as though she may have gotten the message. I was never sure. Shortly afterwards, I retired from my position at the hospital, and therefore no longer met with individual or groups, losing touch with her and others.

One day I returned from Germany where I had been visiting for a few weeks. A call was on my answering service to call the CEO of a local hospital. When I called, the director she said, "I have sad news, and good news. One of your dear friends who used to be in one of your groups has died. How ever, I want you to know that before her death she called me to her bedside and asked, "Where is Dr. Doty?" I told her that you were out of the country, and she replied, "Please do me this favor, wherever he is, contact him and tell him, "Thank you, thank you for loving me and my family and tell him I will never forget him."

Oh God, the tears and more tears, tell my response better than any words. From that day to this one, I have despaired of self-flagellation, and realized the danger of the inner critic, sometimes so damaging that even the love of God can not penetrate. A ray of light comforts me. I was close to her children and they seem to have gotten her quiet gentleness and her love of nature. For that I felt comforted and grateful.

Retirement Years

The Joy of Giving

I waited for the doors of the department store to open and turned to my left to pick up a cart. As I approached the carts, someone pushed a cart to me and said, with a lilt in her voice and a big smile, "Good morning to you, sir. I hope you have a nice day."

I looked into a wrinkled face with shining eyes and thought, how can she do this all day long. She looks like she is at least in her late 70s.

I placed my hand on her arm and said, "Bless you. What a smile and what a greeting!. I'll bet after eight hours of this you'll feel like saying, 'Go jump in the lake' to the next customer."

Her eyes opened wider, her face lit up and she said, "Oh no, sir. These are the happiest hours of my day. It gives meaning to my life. I can bring a little joy to other people's lives, and I can forget my aches and pains and my loneliness. When I get home and have my bath and my supper and watch a little TV, I go to bed thankful that tomorrow will bring another day of meaning to my life."

"Well, I'll tell you one thing," I said, "You've helped to make a better day for me, and I'm appreciative." As I pushed my cart away, I heard her happy voice, "And good morning to you, ma'am."

That night before going to sleep, I remembered that smiling face and wondered how old that woman was. I decided to ask her the next time I went to that store. A few days later, I went through the door and there she was. When she greeted me with her cheerful smile and her warm greeting, I asked her, "How old are you?" She said, "I'm seventy-nine going on eighty."

"I can't believe you can do this for eight hours." "Oh yes," she answered. "I don't have to do this. It brings me joy."

And it also brings joy to people like me, every time I see your smiling face and hear your warm greeting."

"You've made my day," she said.

Oatmeal Cookies

I had been in the ministry for more than sixty years, and had experienced a lot of surprises, but none more so than a call I received one morning from a woman who had been a teenager in my youth group many years before. I recognized her voice immediately. She wasted no time. "I have a question for you. You may think it strange, and I'm embarrassed to ask, but I don't know who to else to ask. I knew you would be honest with me."

"And what is your question?"

"Do you believe in oral sex?"

I'll admit I was surprised and a bit taken aback. But I slowly recovered and said approximately these words. "Thank you for remembering me after all these years and believing that I would be honest with you. I can't give you a 'yes or no' answer, but here goes: There are many ways that men and women the world over express their love to each other and it varies with the culture. The Eskimos rub noses and that apparently turns them on. One man told me that his greatest excitement came when his wife touched his feet with her feet. Another said that when his wife kissed him in his ear, he experienced an orgasm. Some men are turned on by big breasts; others by small breasts. Some women like men with big buttocks. So to say "yes or no" is inadequate. No one should generalize how people should express their love. I don't believe in extreme things like tying people to a bedpost, whipping them with leather straps, damaging the flesh as ways of exciting people sexually. To me that is not love. Whatever methods you employ are acceptable as long as they are mutually acceptable (that is a must) and bring joy and do not harm the body, I see no problem with that. Most important of all is that you love each other and bring pleasure to each other, whether it is a love note, a gentle touch, a kind deed, or sexual intercourse. That's a long answer, but that's my answer.

She responded quickly, "Thank you, thank you, so much. I knew you would be honest with me. I have no money to send, but I'll make you some oatmeal cookies and send them right away."

I end this story with two comments. My seminary training never prepared me for questions like that. And the oatmeal cookies were delicious.

Black Man in the Twin Cities

When I was a child in Old Hickory, Tennessee, Negroes were referred to as "niggers", a derogatory term for most. In our home the right term was "Negra", and that was not a derogatory term for us. Through the years other words have been used like Negro (used most often by Martin Luther King, Jr.), Blacks and Afro-Americans. Clearly the word "nigger" is the no-no word and after that the right choice of words is not clear.

Recently I was in Minneapolis and was standing by my car in a parking lot. A black man approached wearing a T-shirt with the word Tarheels written in bold letters. (It is a word referring to the University of North Carolina Athletic teams.) Teasing him, I said, I'm a Duke man, myself (a classic rivalry exists between Duke University and North Carolina). The man laughed and we began small talk. I abruptly changed the subject, "By the way, I am going South soon visiting lots of civil rights places like the King Center and Selma, Alabama, and I want to know what is the preferred word when referring to you guys?"

"Well, I'll tell you one thing for sure, I'm no Afro-American, I'm an American; and I frankly don't care what you call me, it is the way you treat me that matters to me."

For three weeks I traveled all through North Carolina, South Carolina, Georgia and Alabama, visiting schools, churches, restaurants, motels, museums, Universities, police stations, and people's residences. In referring to certain individuals or groups, I rarely heard the words Blacks or Negroes. Has progress been made? Quite a lot, you think, if your skin is white. Some, but a long way to go, if your skin is black.

Cats

When I was a boy, I used to go hunting with my dad and my brother. We hunted for rabbits, squirrels, quail and doves. I enjoyed the time with my father because his work load was heavy and I didn't see him a lot.

The hunting was a "mixed bag" for me; because I felt sorry for the little animals, especially the quail and the doves. They were so soft, so beautiful, so helpless.

Often we would run across cats that had gone wild and lived in the woods. My father always shot them. He said they destroyed the game birds and other birds as well. Also, gangs of boys in our neighborhood were mean to cats and no one that I knew had a cat in the house. Cats were low on the totem pole.

Dogs were treated with more respect and valued for their hunting skills. A few people had dogs in their houses, and cherished them as pets. I was caught up in that culture and couldn't imagine wanting a cat for a pet. I didn't like how they were mistreated, however, and attempted to protect them when they were harmed.

Many years later my wife and I heard a cat meowing on our porch outside a sliding glass door. My wife finally opened the drapes and said, "The poor little thing is really hungry. Can't we give it a little milk?"

The cat was thin and pitiful looking, and we invited him in. Kathy fetched some milk and he gulped it down. Then, he purred and purred and rubbed against our legs. We decided to take him to a local vet to see if he needed any shots or medicine. We put a notice in the lost and found in the local paper with our telephone number, as well as the vet's, and thought some child would call for it, and be ‹thrilled to have its lost pet back home again. About a week and a few days later the vet telephoned and said that no one had called and they couldn't keep the cat any longer and would have to put him down. We looked at each other and with one voice said, "Let's go get him!"

Neither of us had ever had a cat before, but we fell in love with our new arrival. We agreed from the beginning that we wouldn't attempt to teach him tricks or change him in any way. He was to be our teacher in the ways of cats. And what a joy it has been! We both loved dogs—golden retrievers, boxers, poodles, black labs, collies, German shepherds—but Bib, our first cat, was a new experience. He had a white bib-like streak under his chin, and that's why we called him Bib. When he became an adult, he became Mr. Bib.

From the very beginning we put him on a leash and took long walks in the neighborhood, and after a few days of getting used to it he loved it. The neighbors were surprised to see a cat on a leash, and he became everyone's friend. He especially loved children, and they enjoyed his purring attention.

Like most cats, Bib loved to cuddle, to be combed, to play with his toys, and he brought a kind of delight to us that only a cat can bring. He slept on our bed, of course, to his delight and ours.

He did so many things that brought us joy. I play a harmonica, and the moment I began to play, he would run into the room, jump up into my lap and try to get his mouth into the harmonica. We enjoyed sharing that little experience with our four-legged friend.

Bib did not like to travel in the car, and he whined and fought it when we put him in the car. At times, when we went to the lake, he had to go with us, and it was painful for him and for us. One day we played some symphony music on the car radio, and he immediately calmed down. He was okay for the rest of the trip and we were stunned. On the return trip home, he began to scratch and whine, and we remembered. So, with fear and trembling, we turned on the car radio and sure enough, Mr. Bib lay down in the back seat of the car, and enjoyed the concert.

Are you beginning to like Mr. Bib? Well you would if you had known him. We think he was an angel in his former life. He sure was in this life. He gave us so much. He's gone now, but he will always live in our hearts. And now we have two more four-legged angels, "Georgie and Tucker".

Martin Luther King said, "The white people don't like us, because they don't know us." Mr. Bib would agree with Dr, King. "They don't like us, because they don't know us." If you've never owned a cat, you "ain't lived yet." Right, cat owners?

Fishing Guide

A friend was a guide for persons who wanted to spend part, or all of their vacation on a canoe trip in the Superior National Forest (Boundary Waters) and into the Quetico (Canada lake country bordering the U.S.) Bill had been a guide since he was thirteen years of age. He knew the Boundary Waters like he knew his own backyard. He loved his life as a guide, was an excellent fisherman and a superb outdoor cook. He was also a good storyteller. Many people requested him for their guide for these reasons.

One industrialist from the Twin Cities was sitting around the campfire the night before his vacation was over. He was already dreading returning to the city. He knew he would miss the starry skies, the sound of lapping water, the cool breezes, the call of the wild. He also knew he would miss his guide and his way of life. He waited until the fire burned down and all the campers were ready for sleep, and then he approached Bill.

"Bill," he said, "How would you like to come to the Twin Cities and go to work for me? I will pay you a good salary."

Bill was quiet for a moment, and then answered, "But I already have a job."

The man continued, "With the salary I will pay you, you can buy a nice home in the city."

Bill butted in saying, "I already have a nice home on a small lake, and I can see the stars at night and listen to the sounds of the loons and the barn owls and the wind in the pines."

The man pressed on, "But Bill, I would give you at least three weeks vacation and you could come up hear and enjoy it,"

"I'm already enjoying it," Bill interrupted.

Then Bill looked the man in the eye and said, "Thank you so much, but you see, I'm already here for fifty-two weeks of the year, and nothing you would pay me would be worth leaving this place that I love so much."

Both men sat quietly and then the "city man" said, "Yes, you are home, Bill. You are truly at home."

Appreciation

We received a letter from President Clinton, asking for help with personal debts due to lawyer's fees. My wife and I discussed the situation and decided we wanted to send a check.

Some time later, we received a phone call from someone in the Twin Cities asking, "Reverend Doty, I understand you sent a check to President Clinton recently to help him with his debts."

"That's correct."

"Can you tell me why you, as a retired minister, would do this?"

As I write this story, I cannot believe I did not ask the caller who he was and why he wanted to know, but I did not.

I replied, in so many words, "The answer is very simple. He asked us for help, and we decided we would like to share as best we could."

We felt President Clinton had made some very poor decisions with his sex life, but that was not the whole story. He had done some great things as our president, including reducing the national debt, showing real concern for the black community, and for working tirelessly for many months to bring peace to the Middle East, to mention a few.

Furthermore, I know myself well enough to know I have made some big mistakes in my life, and needed some loving support when I was down. I certainly do not want to be judged by my mistakes alone. Thank God, I have received my share of TLC (tender loving care.) during my lifetime.

I wish we had been able to send a bigger check to express our appreciation for President Clinton's presidency. If I have it correctly, former President Clinton and Carter are the two most respected Americans in the world today. Not to appreciate a most human, human being, would be to deny the possibility of great goodness in all of us, inspite of our ever present flaws.

There was no response from the other end of the line. Only the click of the receiver.

To Say Goodbye

It was late in the afternoon, and I was about ready to stop writing stories about my ministry, when there was a knock on the door. When I opened it, a young man, in his mid-twenties, slightly bent, hat in hands said, "May I come in?"

"Sure, Bill, come in, its good to see you" This young man had attended a young people's group I had agreed to lead in the church we were attending. He was always very quiet, and I was surprised he would drop by so unexpectedly.

Bill was pale, and obviously really upset. He dropped his hat on the floor and clasped his hands on his head. "I came to say good-bye."

"Well, I appreciate your coming by. Where are you going?"

He couldn't seem to get the words out, even though his mouth was open. "Take your time, Bill. I'm in no hurry."

Tears began to fall on his cheeks and he blurted out, "I'm going to die, and I wanted to say good-bye before I go."

I took him by the arm and led him into the living room, found comfortable chairs for us both and gently eased him down, bringing my chair close to him.

"What makes you think you are going to die?" I managed to ask.

Tears began to fall on his cheeks and he blurted out, "I'm going to take my life and I wanted to say thank you for all you've meant to me before I go."

He began to shake, more tears came, and I managed to ask, " Can you tell me why you think you have to end your life?"

"Yes, I can tell you. You see, where I work there is this woman, and she is such a wonderful person. She's beautiful and she's kind to me and everyone likes her."

And then he stopped, and seemed to have difficulty with the next words. Finally I said, "Go on, Bill."

He continued, "I think about her a lot, especially at night, when I'm in bed—and one night I —"

He could not go on, so I responded, "I can certainly understand that."

He blurted out, "Yeah, but she's married!"

"So?"

"So", and the tears came again, as he continued, "God can never forgive me, I know he can't."

I took his hands and said, "Bill, why did you tell me this?"

"Because, well, I knew you would understand—I knew you wouldn't hate me," and then he sobbed.

"Look at me," I finally said, and added, "You are 100% correct. I do understand, and I am so grateful that you shared this beautiful person with me. She sounds like a rare human being, one that would be so easy to want to be close to." I continued, "And your response seems most natural to me."

A faint smile crossed his face, but he said nothing.

"I do understand, but your God doesn't understand, does he? Your God is too small. He isn't as loving as I am. He isn't as loving as you are, and He is a long way from being as loving as Jesus of Nazareth. You need to let this judgmental God go."

There were no words from Bill, but deep breaths, like sighs of relief, and I spoke again. "Bill, would you be willing to stay here with Kathy and me, and spend the night? And if you feel better, you can go home in the morning."

Without hesitation, Bill said, "Yes, I think I would like that."

I knew Kathy liked Bill. I went in to the kitchen to talk to her, briefly explained the situation and asked her if she would be willing to have him stay the night. She readily agreed.

We had very recently moved into the house and it was still a mess. The beds were not even assembled, and we would all need to sleep on the floor. The food would not be the Waldorf, but probably slim pickins, but that didn't seem important. What was important was that we shared with each other. We talked until late that evening and finally gave in to our need for rest and get some sleep.

The next morning, Kathy and I were awakened by sounds from the kitchen. Bill was up, preparing breakfast from whatever he could find. I don't remember the specifics. I do remember that he left after breakfast and returned later in the day with gifts—a book of poetry for Kathy, and a red rose for me. He knew what we each loved him.

Bill is happily married today, and he and his wife have a wonderful family. I don't know what he remembers about this story, but I do know that he has let go the angry, judgmental God, and I know Kathy and I will always remember that special evening together.

Angel Nurse

We were just beginning to really enjoy our retirement, finding time to spontaneously drop everything, and do something fun when Kathy was called by the office of the Virginia Piper Research Institute in Minneapolis. She had volunteered to be a part of a research project to learn more about the causes of ovarian, colon and lung cancer. Because Kathy's father had died of colon cancer, she thought she'd like to be a part of such research, both for herself and for others.

The call was made to inform her that from the tests that were made before the project began, it was discovered that an ovarian cyst on one of her ovaries looked as thought it were about to metastasize, and surgery was advised as soon as possible.

Naturally, we were dismayed, checked it out with a gynecologist who was a good friend, and he said, "Don't delay." Our plans to "drop everything and have fun" had to be postponed and we made an appointment for the surgery.

After the surgery we learned that cancer did not appear, the cyst had been removed, and we were enormously relieved.

However, Kathy told me later that when she came to after the surgery, she opened her eyes, looked at the door to the bathroom and saw a bag hanging on the door knob, 'Chemotherapy waste', and realized she was in the cancer ward. She was stunned. So, she thought, I do have cancer, and the tears started to flow.

When I visited Kathy later in the day she greeted me with a smile on her face. "It was worth waking up in the cancer ward, just to meet my nurse. Fred, the best way to describe her is to say, 'She is an angel!' Kathy's gratitude for her nurse's care was so profound, that I looked for her in order to express my appreciation. When I told her what Kathy had said, she replied without hesitation, "Yes, Mr. Doty, I am an angel and that's what I am here for." In a way, I was stunned at her quite definite response, even though I had noticed an "angel" pin on her uniform. I hugged her and told her we wouldn't forget her. Then I went in search of Kathy's doctor and asked him why he had put Kathy in the oncology ward, when her cyst was not cancerous. I said, "You scared us to death."

"I'm sorry," he said. "I can see why you were worried. I was not at all sure the cyst had not metastasized, and had to reserve a place for her in the cancer ward in case it had. But mostly, I wanted your wife to have the very best after care available, and the nurse in this ward is an absolute angel. I wanted her to be Kathy's caregiver."

Later in the day one of my daughters called to ask about Kathy. I shared the story about Kathy's nurse. Her reply was again a surprise. She said simply, "Why are you so surprised? I feel I am an angel also in the work that I do every day," and added, "You, too are an angel, if you only knew it." And this last line is for you who read it.

"You are an angel, too, if you only knew it."

My Mother

The most important person in my life, and I have rarely mentioned her name in all these stories. I am surprised and perplexed. One simple story may share her essence.

It was the night after my high school graduation, the night of the farewell dance. It was a big night for me and all of my classmates. As I started out the door, I said to my father, and mother, "I'll be late tonight."

My father immediately replied, "The door will be locked at 10 P.M."

"But, dad, the grand march isn't until eleven o'clock, and as class president, I am to lead it."

"I think you have ears and can hear. "The door will be locked at 10 P.M."

I could hardly believe my ears; and yet, I knew there was no recourse, so I said, "I will not be home before ten o'clock.

I was half in tears, and angry, but immediately began to problem solve my dilemma. The first thought that came to me: You can sleep on a church pew. You know where the key is hidden. (I was the church custodian.)

A great evening with my classmates, whom I dared not tell my situation—and now for my substitute bed. I opened the church basement window and found a waiting pew. It was hard and uncomfortable, but I gave it a try. I couldn't sleep, the "holy spirit" idea was a little spooky. I finally gave up, and headed home.

When got home I went around to the back of our house, hoping I could find a way inside. When I got closer to the house, I saw my mother's face through a basement window. She had been waiting for me. She opened the door quietly, pointed to an old couch, and left me for a decent night's sleep.

This was never mentioned to my father. My mother was walking a tightrope between her caring for me and my needs, and not wanting to alienate her husband. But, for me, she could do it. That was my mother, always there when the going was rough, almost never critical, available to listen when I needed to talk, supportive of my dreams, and the head of my cheering section until the day she died.

She was a light, a candle that forever burns in my life.

I know what love is; for sure, a mother's love.

Waitress

Somewhere near the year 2000 the church which we were attending held a public meeting celebrating our acceptance of homosexuals into the full life of our church. It was an evening meeting and a large crowd was not anticipated; however, the time arrived for the service to begin, the sanctuary was almost filled. The committee which planned the ecumenical service asked me to say a few words.

This was not to be a big speech and I was not asked to do this until after I arrived. One thing I remember saying was that I thought that every person on earth was unique, like none other in history—never before and never again. Each person reflected a part of the creator that no other person revealed, and each person gave each of us an opportunity to experience another part of the creator.

At the close of the service a young woman (about twenty years of age) literally ran up to me, eyes wide open, big smile on her face, blurted out, "Thank you, thank you, thank you for believing that God is in me in a unique way."

A few weeks later my wife and I were seated at a restaurant looking at the menu when a young waitress came to our table to take our order. She suddenly recognized me and announced, "He's the one who thinks I have a unique gift from God. I'm so happy to be your waitress."

The world is full of people who do not feel good about themselves. Many are filled with self hate and an increasing number commit suicide rather than live. Unfortunately they do not feel that anyone cares about them. One person can often change that with a kind word, a gentle touch, or a helping hand. One person.

And a Little Child Shall Lead Them

Christmas Gifts

It was early in December and the congregation was making plans to prepare Christmas boxes for families in need. Through the Salvation Army we received family cards, identifying how many members and their ages. Church families could select a family and select gifts of clothing, toys for the kids, food, etc. My wife and I felt very awkward about not accepting a family because we had already discussed our dilemma of not having resources to prepare Christmas for our four small daughters. Sorrowfully, we did not take a card with a family to prepare for Christmas. Fortunately all the cards were taken by parishioners.

After Sunday dinner one of our daughters said, "Mom and Dad, we need to have a family conference." This was not an unusual request so we gathered in the living room. Our twelve-year-old spoke for the four sisters. "We know that money is tight this year and that you two are worried about our Christmas gifts. Well, we don't need anything and we would much rather give gifts to people who really need them. So, we took a card this morning and we want to give gifts to a needy family." The oldest said, "I can baby sit and use that money." Each of the other three said I can give my best doll or I can give my music box, and on they went. We were understandably in tears, and so we said, if that is what you want we'll do anything we can to help.

Would you believe it was the best Christmas any of us could remember? And of course some family member had sent some gifts for the girls. But the greatest gifts they received were the ones they gave away.

Christmas Eve

It was Christmas Eve and the sanctuary was filled, with extra chairs placed in the narthex. All ages were present including the children. It was time for children to come forward and place their gifts at the foot of the manger scene. As you can guess, the adults were enjoying watching the antics connected with the children coming down the long aisle, some walking, others skipping, and some even running. The various expressions on their faces told many stories, much laughter and some tears.

Suddenly, there was a problem. A small boy was being slightly pushed by his father to go forward and place his gift on the now pile of gifts at the foot of the manger scene. The mother of the child was up front with the choir. After much coaxing the little boy came forward; and when reaching the manger scene, he threw down his gift in apparent disgust. The congregation was hysterically laughing and the mother was of course horrified.

There is more to come. The little boy turned around and walked down two steps and headed to his seat in the rear of the sanctuary. But suddenly, he turned around, ran back up the steps, grabbed his gift and headed for his seat with the speed of lightening. And the congregation was out of control with laughter. When the congregation was finally under control I said, "Even the angels in heaven are rejoicing with us."

Maybe he thought, "The baby Jesus has enough gifts. What about me?"

I Know You!

My wife and I were invited to have dinner in one of our parishioners' home. We arrived at the appointed hour and our host was not quite ready. She said, "Oh, I'm so sorry; we're never on time, but please come in." She was trying to feed her two children, ages about five or seven, both boys. I volunteered to feed them and we had a ball. I used various unorthodox methods to finally get the food from their plates into their stomachs. After a while the mother appeared all beautifully dressed and seeing the empty plates remarked: "How did you do it; we'll put you on regular."

It was a delightful evening. That was Saturday night and the next morning was children's Sunday. Children stayed in the sanctuary with their parents for a few minutes then on the second hymn left for their classes.

The ushers had seated the worshipers and all the children were seated in the front rows. I walked in wearing a full length black robe, ascended the stairs to the pulpit and started to say the call to worship. The sanctuary was stone silent. A small boy, age five—one of the two I had "conned" the night before into eating his peas and carrots—jumped to his feet and yelled, "Hey, I know you!" After an instantaneous roar of laughter, I remarked, "Yeah, and I know you."

His final remark was a resounding "YEAH!" Frankly, his call to worship was so much more engaging than the one I had prepared.

Bob Mowers

When I was a boy growing up in Old Hickory, Tennessee my family attended a Methodist church and it was a very important part of our lives. The bishop of the conference decided how long the minister would stay in a local parish, usually about four years. I didn't like that. About the time you really got to know and care about your leader, he was moved to another parish.

When I became a clergyman it took me two or three years just to get to know my congregation. The thought of leaving in four years would have been terribly frustrating. Fortunately in my last parish I spent thirteen wonderful years.

As you can imagine those thirteen years were filled with precious memories—some painful ones also, like the death of a child or a service man killed in the line of duty. Even after leaving a congregation, relationships did not cease. Letters would come telling of joys and sorrows, bringing delight and sorrow across the country.

One former parishioner died recently from a long and extremely painful illness and he was ready to be freed from the agonizing pain. He was a truly remarkable man and he and his beloved wife had spent years working with high school young people and were much adored by them. Shortly after his death his children and his grandchildren made a list of things that dad/daddy/Grandpa/Bompa taught through the years with his words, actions, and deeds. His wife knew how much that list would mean to me. It brought back so many memories and once more made me realize how fortunate I have been. I read the list over and over again, and called and asked permission to share the things "Bompa" had said.

She said, "Anyway you choose to use it, Bob would be delighted." I've saved the list until now. It seems the right time.

What Dad Taught Us

• Always call your wife your "bride" no matter how many years you have been married.

• Always show your best work: never do anything "half-assed".

• Speak your mind but accept the consequences of your words.

• Always eat together as a family; fill the table with love and laughter and an extra seat for whoever may wander in.

• Let your life be seen through your actions as much as through your words.

• Joke with those you love and laugh when you are the center of the joke.

• Your word is your commitment. Do not make promises lightly.

• Don't take tomorrow's challenges on your heart today.

• Expand your community continuously.

• Be available to listen.

• Dad's danger signs: middle names, red ears, the snap of his fingers.

• There is always a place and a time for practical jokes: everyplace and all the time.

• Never be afraid to cry at the sight of beautiful art, the sound of beautiful music, or the memory of a beautiful moment.

• Set clear parameters of expected behavior but be prepared to forgive regularly and often.

• Seek new challenges.

• Yes, Scott, There is "right" and there is "wrong".

• LOVE LOVE LOVE LOVE LOVE LOVE.

Rules to Follow

Beth lived in a wonderful family where she was loved and appreciated. It was a family where there were rules to follow, rules that were understood by each person, the rules having been carefully explained by both parents. One day Beth broke one of those rules much to her mother's surprise. Beth was not known to be a rule breaker, in fact, just the opposite. Her mother said to Beth, "You know what the rules are and you know the consequences, so when your father comes home, he will be told and you will suffer the consequences."

Beth was not belligerent or sarcastic. She simply replied, "I know, Mom."

She went out into the backyard and climbed up the steps of an old ladder to the roof of a small barn. She lay there watching the clouds high in the sky. It was one of Beth's favorite things to do when she wanted to be alone and quiet. She lost all sense of time with her preoccupation with the unusual cloud formations.

After a while her father came home from work and her mother told him about Beth's breaking of the rule. He came out the back door and soon saw her on the roof of the old barn. As he approached the barn Beth saw him coming and yelled to him, "Hurry, Dad, I have something to show you."

Her father hurried up the ladder and immediately responded in wonder at the magnificent sky and the heavenly cloud formations. Their mutual fascination with the clouds was interrupted when Beth's mother called them to supper. Beth and her dad came into the house arm in arm with joy on their faces. Naturally Beth's mother was curious. After supper Beth was upstairs with her homework and her mother was listening to her dad explain what happened on the roof. She said to her husband after he finished his explanation, "Sometimes there are things more important than the consequences of breaking rules."

Hell Dammit, Daddy

One Monday morning—my day away from the parish—little Mary came running to me crying. "Hell dammit, Daddy" and she was carrying her precious doll in her hands in two pieces.

"Hell dammit; it must be awfully bad."

"Yes, yes, Daddy, my dolly's head is broken."

I slipped the body back into the socket and handed her the dolly all fixed again. The happy smile mixed with tears were my reward topped off with "thank you so much dear Dad."

I thought about those words all week, "Hell dammit, Daddy." First of all, where did she get them? Her mother and I didn't use those words. The only "no-no " word I used occasionally (and in private of course) was "oh shit." Nevertheless, there they were, right out of nowhere and quite expressive in that awful situation. "Hell" wasn't enough nor "dammit" wasn't enough, but putting the two together was just right. She couldn't have defined the words, but she felt that the situation called for them.

Had I used those words as a child I would not have gotten off so easily. The broken doll would have been lost and the no-no words would have taken front stage. Eventually the dolly would have been fixed, but another lesson would have been blurred or lost. The words, more important than the broken dolly and a broken heart.

As the week wore on I simply couldn't forget those words, those tears, that desperate look and, of course, the resurrection of "thank you dear Dad."

And so the sermon for Sunday was changed and the sign out in front of the church was changed. Sunday's sermon title was changed for all to see as they rode by, "HELL DAMMIT DADDY."

I'm sure there were a few who thought the title inappropriate, but the overall response was positive, and I hope some parents put the emphasis on the right syllable. Jesus would have understood and approved—I think—for he did say, "Man was not made for the Sabbath, but the Sabbath was made for man," interpreted to mean, "Better to pick an ear of corn on the Sabbath if one is hungry than to go hungry for twenty-four hours".

Four-Letter Words

For some reason the rules didn't seem to always apply to men and on occasion my father or one of my uncles would come out with "damn it" or "shit." We kids would always be surprised, but we didn't say anything. Sometimes we would laugh a little, but we didn't let our father see us laugh. And usually the men didn't cuss in front of the women.

I used to wonder why all the fuss about a few little four letter words, but then my mother would quote scripture to reinforce her rules and that did make me think twice about using the forbidden words, even in private. Her favorite scripture was from James 5:12. I knew it by heart, "But above all, my brethren, do not swear, either by heaven or by earth or with any other oath but let your 'yes be yes' and your 'no be no' that you may not fall under condemnation."

I must admit that was pretty heavy for one little four-letter word. Of all the words that I dared not use were the "f" word and taking the Lord's name in vain (God damn it) because that may mean "roasting in hell." I did hear the "f" word a few times but never the other words. I rarely used the four letter words, and I never used the extreme words. I didn't seem to need them, but I thought a lot about taking the Lord's name in vain. I couldn't imagine God burning anyone in hell for saying those words. Mom didn't say "for sure" but one was in danger of hellfire. I became possessed with the idea. I simply had to know.

One night I went down to the corner where there was a street light. No one was around and I thought "now or never." So I spit the words out as quickly as I could and very softly. I waited for some divine retaliation and nothing happened. I thought maybe God didn't hear me so I ventured once more, and this time more slowly and a little clearer. I waited and waited and still—nothing. All of a sudden I let her rip, "God damn it, God damn it, God damn it," and still nothing. I HAD THEM! I had been conned. But what could I do about it. I couldn't tell my mother. It would break her heart and I dearly loved my mother. If I told my father it would surely mean a licking so I smugly carried my little secret telling no one. It was a secret between me and God.

With my own children we didn't make such a big deal about four letter words though they knew I didn't like the "f" word so, of course, that's the one that was used when one of the girls was mad at me, her "ace in the hole" of course. It seemed to me that any extreme reaction on my part was worse than the "f" word.

If I have any advice it is to model the language you want your children to use, learn to handle your anger and you won't need the no-no words and respond with understanding when someone blurts out with a no-no word. Maybe, "I'm sorry you are hurting" and a gentle hug is worth a try.

Dates with Daughters

One of the negative things about being a clergyman is that your work never seems to end. No matter how much I did, I was always aware of what was left undone. If one also is cursed by a need to please—which I was—then the work becomes even more difficult. In my last parish I found myself working late and getting up early in an attempt to get more done. The problem persisted, of course. The problem was not the parish, but the problem was Fred.

My greatest regret in all that was how little time I spent with my children. In one of those guilty moments, I made date with each one of my girls. I said, "It will be an evening out for just you and me. You decide what we will do."

One daughter said, "I want you to take me to an amusement park in Long Beach (maybe seventy-five miles each way)."

Another one said, "I want to sleep out under the stars in the woods at Lake Arrowhead (100 miles each way)."

A third one said, "I want to go out to dinner at a certain restaurant and order anything I want." This story is about the oldest daughter (ten or twelve) who wanted to go to the amusement park. When we parked our car and entered the park, Navy men in uniform were everywhere and some were drinking freely and loud and boisterous. She held on to my hand very tightly.

She really loved it. Lots of rides, side shows, games of chance, many food booths and tons of people having fun. We went on the roller coaster and one other ride. She had cotton candy and a hot dog and a coke. I didn't limit her. She limited herself, fully aware that our family budget was tight.

On the way back, she was "full of it", talking a mile a minute. At some point she said, "Dad, you haven't said one word since we left Long Beach."

Then she laughed and said, "But I haven't stopped talking, have I?"

We both laughed and she began again. Before we got home she was suddenly asleep and stayed asleep until we arrived home. Her mother was awake and eager to hear a report on her night out with dad. She laughed and laughed as she gave mom a full report.

She got ready for bed, and we listened to her prayers and said good night. A few minutes later she came into our bedroom and said, "Dad, do you mind if I sleep in your bedroom tonight? I can sleep beside your bed on the floor in my sleeping bag."

You can guess my answer. One hand up from the sleeping bag and one hand down from the bed. We went to sleep holding hands. That moment was cherished and will forever be—a reminder that if we are too busy to find time for our children, we are too busy and our values are skewed!

Mary's Prayers

It was bedtime and Mary was on her knees beside her bed ready to say her prayers; but from the length of her prayers not ready to go to sleep. She asked God to bless her friends, her teachers, all the poor people, and the hungry. By this time, my knees were getting tired. Mary was very specific about her family, "God bless my mommy, God bless my dear Molly, God bless little Martha, and God bless my daddy, who tries so hard to be good."

She paused for a moment as if to get the next words just right and added, "And dear God, what are we going to do with Margaret?" (Margaret was the free one among our children.)

When I got up off my aching knees and kissed Mary "good night" I was a bit troubled at her observations, at her childlike wisdom. I couldn't forget those words, "Bless my daddy who tries so hard to be good." (I wasn't sure she thought that I was making it.) I couldn't sleep. Thoughts poured through my head like; better that I be more real, more honest about my dishonesty, better that I recognize and show my anger, better that I share my frustrations rather than my unrealistic optimism. Yes, better because it would create a climate where my children could accept their anger and their frustrations without guilt and without the fear of hurting 'dear dad.' Better for everyone.

O God, we thank you for our children, for their refreshing openness, for their wide eyed openness, for their quickness to anger, or laughter or tenderness, for their unabashed tears and their readiness to forgive. We thank you for a second chance for us to grow up with them as our teachers. Amen.

Say It With Your Eyes

I was working with a close friend in a psychological clinic in southern California. One day he shared the following story. He had been seeing a child in counseling and had invited the child's mother to come into the counseling room with her son. The mother seemed anxious and all of a sudden blurted out to her son, "Tell Dr. —— that mommy loves you."

Without hesitation the little boy said, "Mommy, say it with your eyes."

The story hit me hard—right in the gut. The little boy had shared a truth that so many children have felt but never verbalized. It reminded me of a poem a child had written, one I could never forget. It was entitled "someone" and goes like this.

And she looked at me saying with her eyes
A lie, like she always said a lie, and I would listen
For truths when I listened to her which was rare
But when I did, I would try to
Hear truths but I would never hear them
I would hear only lies.

Frances Wickes wisely said, "Our children do not hear what we say; they intuit what we are." The painful truth is that we cannot give what we do not have, and we cannot keep what we do have. No amount of "I love you's" can change the fact when a child—or an adult—is not loved. They do not hear the words. They feel only the pain of the lies. Enough said!

Ten Commandments

In the 1960s I taught a lot of classes in bible study after school. I remember one particular group of fifth graders who were studying the Ten Commandments. In the first meeting I told them some simple things like the commandments could be found in both books of Exodus and Deuteronomy, that they were a supreme factor in the age long process of keeping people living together honestly and fairly for thousands of years and that the ideas were contained in other religions also.

Then each child sat in quiet and read the Ten Commandments and tried to decide which each one thought was the most important. They were literally excited about the process as they were reading. I was guessing which commandment they would choose. I was almost sure which one it would be, "Thou shalt not kill." Is that what you guessed? Well, to my genuine surprise it was clearly, "Thou shalt honor thy Father and thy Mother."

I am still surprised at my response to them which was, "Ah, come on, you can be honest with me, what do you really think?"

One little boy responded as quick as the blink of an eye, "We have to have that or we are in real trouble, aren't we Reverend?"

His sincerity upended me and I said quietly, "You are so right, we do need to have that."

There were only a few minutes left, and I asked if there were any questions, and there was one, "What is adultery?"

"Does anyone know?" I asked, and no one knew; so I suggested they ask their parents and report back to me at the next class. When the next class began and I asked for their parents' explanation, without an exception the parents said, "Ask Reverend Doty."

I had been outmaneuvered, and I laughed and they laughed. I explained to them simply "adultery is when a married man or woman makes love with someone whom they are not married to." Once more with the speed of an arrow, the same little boy in his delightful English accent spoke up, "Oh my, we simply mustn't have that, must we."

This delightful story reveals the delight I have had through the years in teaching children and being taught by children.

Broken Promise

I opened the back door to take a walk in the back yard and my little daughter came running to me all upset. I kneeled down to meet her eye to eye and reached out to put my arms around her; but she pulled away from me and said in tears, "I'm so mad at you daddy and I hate you too."

"Oh, my goodness, and it hurts inside too when you're mad, doesn't it?"

"Yes, yes, it does hurt. Want to know why I hate you so much?"

"Oh, yes, I do, I really do want to know because it hurts you so much and it hurts me too when you are hurting."

"I'm sorry, Dad, but you remember when you said you would take me to the new park and push me in the swing. I waited and waited a long time and you never took me."

The tears came again as she said, "You broke your promise."

"Oh, darling, I'm so sorry; I'm very sorry. Daddy should not have broken his promise. I want to keep my promise this very day. This is my day off from the church and we can go to the park as soon as we have our breakfast."

Her little face offered a smile, she jumped up and down in delight and said, "Dear Dad, I love you so much."

May I translate! "I hate you so much means I love you so much it is okay to tell you the truth."

Broken promises to children can be very painful, especially if they happen often. They can erode trust and diminish self worth. Promises kept, build trust, increase self esteem and enrich relationships with parents and children.

Baraboo Children

I recently spoke to about sixty fifth grade students in Baraboo, Wisconsin. Their teacher had been in the high school youth group in my church in Woodland Hills, California, about forty years ago. She remembered being a teenager in the church when Dr. Martin Luther King, Jr. came to speak to our congregation and she had never forgotten it. She wanted me to come and speak to her fifth grade classes about Dr. King's visit and about my marching with Dr. King in Selma, Alabama, after the horrible "Bloody Sunday". I was quite touched that she had located me on the internet after all those years and that her memories with Dr. King were still a treasure in her memory. Baraboo, Wisconsin, however, was a 500 mile round trip and I didn't readily respond to her request.

Two or three years later one more request came saying "I am retiring this year, and it's always been my dream that you would come before I retire". My wife and I decided it was a must and so I agreed to go. I did attach an "if" however. I will come if your students will write me a letter telling me what they want to learn from my presentation. My teacher friend agreed and soon their letter arrived.

Both my wife and I absolutely overwhelmed with their questions. Rather than talk about their questions, let me share some of them.

Why are blacks so bad and why do white people hate them?
Have you ever seen the Ku Klux Klan?
Were you ever left out because you marched with Dr. King?
Were blacks still treated unfairly after the civil rights act?
Is it a law for white people not to insult Negroes?
Do you think whites should always be nice to blacks?
What is the most proper name for blacks?

What was your favorite experience with Dr. King?
Did Dr. King ever want to use violence?
Did Dr. King have any white friends when he was young?
Did he go to a good school?
Did you ever get blasted by water hoses?
Were you afraid of being hurt when you marched?
Have you ever been harassed by people because they didn't like Martin Luther King, Jr.?

This sampling of the children's questions enables you to understand my excitement about spending time with those remarkable kids. My prepared speech was forgotten after those letters, and I planned my remarks around their questions and mostly told them true stories that tended to address their concerns. In a sentence the time spent with those kids was an unforgettable feast for my wife and for me and from the letters they later wrote, it was a feast for them.

The time with them ended with autographs. They patiently waited in line to have their shoes, their t-shirts, their hands, their foreheads and their notebooks autographed. Bless that teacher for inviting us for that memorable experience and for preparing those youth so richly in understanding and appreciating Dr. King and the civil rights movement.

I end this story with a few words from one of the fifth grader's letters to me after the presentation.

> Dear Dr. Doty: I should have said to you bless your heart when I had the chance. I appreciate your signing my shoe, my shirt and my little piece of paper. You have inspired me to help out if the civil rights act is broken. I would go out and speak my voice just like Dr. King did. Please write back.
> Your friend

Truly a feast for Kathy and me and a ray of hope.

And thank, you, Deri Ament, for inviting me to speak to those angelic children.

Brain Tumor

Leslie was on the roof of the house helping his dad replace some shingles. It was a hot day and Leslie said, "I'm tired, Dad, and I need to lie down."

His dad thought he was "goofing off" and he mildly scolded him. Later his dad checked on him and saw that he really was a tired little boy. The next day Leslie came home from school and told his parents that the teacher was confusing him by making everything double on the blackboard. His parents sensed something was wrong and called his doctor immediately. The diagnosis: "Brain Tumor."

"Oh, God, no—no, anything but that!"

And so began a long and increasingly incapacitating nightmare for Leslie and his parents and his sisters. Leslie was the model patient, never complaining, walking to school—his choice—when the doctor felt he should be driven to school, continuing his classes when the teachers felt it was too much for him, continuing his studies at home when he could no longer attend classes, facing operation after operation with courage and optimism.

His curiosity was unending and he became interested in coin collecting, cut glass, learning a foreign language and Bible stories. His surgeon said that he was his model patient and that Leslie did more for him and his faith than any patient he had ever had. Leslie was treated like a son and he truly loved his doctor.

Leslie was twelve or thirteen when he awoke from his tenth brain operation. He was a thin little guy who was made of special timber. All who knew him held him in almost awesome esteem, and nurses and orderlies and his surgeon spoke openly of their love for him. On this particular morning the surgeon called Leslie's father into his office and said, "Herb, I've got bad news for you."

Herb choked up, fighting the tears asked, "Doc, is he going to die?"

"No, Herb, but he is going blind." The doctor's voice cracked and he said, "I'll tell him if you like."

"No, thank you. He's my son. I'll have to tell him."

After going to the nearby chapel and getting down on his knees and asking for God's strength, Herb returned to Leslie's room. Immediately he said, "Son, I've got bad news for you."

"Dad, am I going to die?"

"No —but— but—but you're going blind," and his eyes flooded with tears.

And Leslie's comment upended his dad for the rest of his life. "Ah dad, don't cry. It's okay. I'm a lucky guy. You love me, mom loves me, my family loves me, my doctor loves me, most important of all Jesus loves me."

Leslie's amazing spirit of acceptance and love permeated all those around him through two more operations and until the day he died. I spent endless hours with Leslie during those long and painful years; and the intimate conversations concerning so much that was precious to him is a treasure that words cannot describe. My hours spent with Leslie, more than anything, deepened my relationship with my brother, Herb, father of Leslie.

Eternal God, whose wisdom we often do not understand, we thank you for the Leslies of our lives. They keep us off-balance. They keep us humble. They haunt us with their gentle responses, their acceptance of their suffering and their remarkable capacity to give to us. Their love and their wisdom seem greater than mom's or dad's, too much for their years. We simply accept it and thank you for that bit of heaven on earth. We need such teachers no matter how young—or how old, to show us the way. Amen.

The Sound of Music

Remember *The Sound of Music*, starring Christopher Plummer, Julie Andrews, the singing nuns and the angelic children, the Trapp Family Singers? How many times have you seen it?

Let me tell you a story.

One day, a long time ago, my choir director at the church I was serving in Woodland Hills, California asked me, "How would you like to go to New York City and see the opening of the film "The Sound of Music", starring Christopher Plummer and Julie Andrews?"

I could tell by his facial expression that he was serious.

I must have been dumbfounded. I can't be sure, because that was a half century ago.

He continued, "We have friends who have an apartment on 5th Avenue, and they are in Europe now, and they have offered us a key."

Unless you think I'm dreaming, let me clarify. You see, my choral director was Bill Lee, perhaps the most recorded voice in Hollywood. It was he who had done the "voice over" for Christopher Plummer in *The Sound of Music*. It was Bill's beautiful voice that we heard, not that of Christopher Plummer in that immortal film. Furthermore, his wife, Ada Beth, was one of the singing nuns.

I'm sure I called my wife, Jane, immediately, and soon we sat down with our four little girls, Mary, Molly, Margaret, and Martha and together considered this amazing offer.

The girls were ecstatic. You see they already had their social security numbers as Bill had used them in choruses for a few of his recordings.

I attempted to discuss the pros and cons of such a long adventure, but no one could hear my concerns. I was worried about the long drive, the more than 6,000 miles, round trip, and having to borrow money for the considerable expenses we would incur, besides the free accommodations. How could we keep time-consuming track of four little girls in New York City? All of these worries, I shared only with my wife. I did not want to burden my children with these concerns.

When the time came to take a family vote, there were six "yeses." I was beginning to see this adventure as a once in a life-time opportunity to have a few weeks, away from ministerial responsibilities, with my family, under heavenly circumstances.

And so, we swiftly began our well thought-out preparations.

Every day along the way, we played games, such as who could identify the most birds, or see and count the most deer, or out of state license plates. We sang songs, told stories, ate lunch in parks, and thought and chattered about the Big City.

New York City, for the family, was one magical moment after the other. Every other moment was, "Look, Dad", "Wow, Mom!", "Hey, you guys," until we were exhausted. Lots of New Yorkers seemed taken by our four wonderful little girls, and they seemed to enjoy stopping and engaging them in conversation.

The Big Moment was seeing the film *The Sound Of Music* on its opening night. Everyone in the audience was excited, and our girls were ecstatic.

After the peak experience of hearing Bill and Ada Beth Lee's voices in this award-winning film, we drove on to New Haven, Connecticut, where Jane and I had attended Yale Divinity School. Our little daughters walked, ran and played on the hallowed ground where their parents had gone to school; to them, a long, long time ago.

We then drove on to Sharon, Massachusetts, a magical New England town where a former staff member of our church was now living. He was in his nineties and had formerly been the editor of Pilgrim Press, our denomination's printing press.

Our reunion was joyful, and he was a super guide for us in his fairyland, filling us in on New England history and introducing us to his favorite restaurants.

In one restaurant he had us seated and then excused himself for a few moments and then returned to the table. Shortly afterwards, a tall waitress appeared, in her hand holding the biggest lobster I had ever seen.

She said, laughing, "You must be Brother Fred. Is this one big enough? If not, we'll bring you a bigger one!"

All four little girls screamed as the waitress dangled the live, squirming lobster in front of us. As the waitress disappeared, the girl's composure reappeared; and if I remember correctly, loved the taste of the supremely edible, melted-butter-covered creature from the deep.

We all relived these magical moments all the way back to California, and none of us will ever forget that special time. It was, perhaps, especially meaningful and redeeming for me, whose absorption in the everlasting demands of the ministry prevented me from having special time with my beloved daughters.

Every time I recall that trip, I hear the "Sound of Music" in my mind, my heart and my soul! And I am filled with gratitude.

Reflection

These stories were carefully chosen to represent to the reader what the ministry is really like, knowing that some of them would have little or no meaning to certain readers.

Just as I put a period to what I thought would be my last story, it occurred to me that many of my parishioners requested prayers that I had written, and so I end my group of stories with a prayer most often asked for—a Christmas prayer:

Christmas Prayer

O God, amidst the darkness of hunger and greed, sickness and prejudice,
  hate and fear,
  dry my tears of pessimism and despair.
  Open my eyes to see beneath the greed—loneliness—
  beneath hate and prejudice—fear.
  Temper my criticisms of others by a clearer look at
  my own imperfections.

At this Christmas season, save me from the folly of attempting to quench loneliness with a frantic search for more things.
  Let not the shadows of greed blind my own capacity to give;
  Let not the darkness of another's hopelessness render me hopeless;
  Let not the mood of despair around me paralyze my own inner resources
for good.

In this season of new hope, reawaken in me the child who sees wonder in simple things, and strengthen in me the growing boy who is not immobilized by failures—my own—or other's and who eagerly seeks a better world.
  Help to emerge in me the mature man who
  seeks not the easy road
  and whose hope rises from an inner vision
  which often shines brightest when clouds are darkest.
  Most of all, this season, free me to give of the love that is within me,
  and to receive the love
  that is all around me.
  Oh God of us all, in this season of wonder and hope
  Be born in me anew.

Acknowledgements

Through the years many people have encouraged me to write down the stories of my experiences in the ministry. Certain close friends kept up the encouragement long after my retirement, until I finally realized these friends were trying to tell me something about the importance of sharing the real life experiences of the Christian ministry, so often misunderstood.

I want to thank my friend Hugh Beaumont who kept nudging me over the years to write them down; and to John Stewart, a parishioner and long time friend, who continually pushed me to write my stories, who read them and made helpful suggestions; to Dr. James Goddard who also read the stories and made suggestions, and wrote a blurb for the back of the book, and to Ian Barbour, who wrote a helpful critique. On one occasion Dr. Barbour said to me, "Fred, you had better write these stories down, for the day will come when you won't remember them."

That night I lay in bed thinking about Dr. Barbour's comment, and the next day I began writing and a flood of memories began to emerge day after day.

I want to thank my four daughters, Mary, Molly, Margaret, and Martha for all they taught me through the years, and for the contributions of their own memories that appear here and there in this book. A specials thanks to my dear daughter, Margaret who read the manuscript from beginning to end and made valuable comments.

And thank you, Karen Turringten, for typing the manuscript and adjusting her schedule so many times to hasten the process for publication.

Appreciation to Dr. Kathryn McCreight, assistant priest at St. John's Episcopal Church and teacher at Albertus Magnus College in New Haven, Connecticut, for reading the manuscript, and making suggestions.

There is no way to express my thanks to my wife, Kathy, who more than anyone expressed her appreciation for the stories of my ministry and encouraged and helped me every step of the way. She read the stories from beginning to end as they unfolded. A number of times, she looked me straight in the eyes and said, "You must publish these stories, for they reveal and preserve a rare ministry, and I fear you do not know how rare a ministry.

And there is no adequate way to thank that endless stream of laymen who joined with me in a common dream, in a never ending search for meaning in sorrow and in joy, in life and in death. So often I was humbled by their going the second (and third) mile, giving beyond their means of time and talent, remaining loyal when they found me hard to take., like the friend who said, "Brother Fred, you know how much we love you; but how much do you think we can take?"

Those blessed souls—children, youth, adults, seniors—everyone. They were my wealth and my joy, and they will feed my soul until the day I die.